Democratic Education and Muslim Philosophy

Nuraan Davids • Yusef Waghid

Democratic Education and Muslim Philosophy

Interfacing Muslim and Communitarian Thought

Nuraan Davids
Department of Education Policy Studies
Stellenbosch University
Stellenbosch, South Africa

Yusef Waghid
Faculty of Education
Stellenbosch University
Stellenbosch, South Africa

ISBN 978-3-030-30055-5   ISBN 978-3-030-30056-2 (eBook)
https://doi.org/10.1007/978-3-030-30056-2

© The Editor(s) (if applicable) and The Author(s), under exclusive licence to Springer Nature Switzerland AG 2019
This work is subject to copyright. All rights are solely and exclusively licensed by the Publisher, whether the whole or part of the material is concerned, specifically the rights of translation, reprinting, reuse of illustrations, recitation, broadcasting, reproduction on microfilms or in any other physical way, and transmission or information storage and retrieval, electronic adaptation, computer software, or by similar or dissimilar methodology now known or hereafter developed.
The use of general descriptive names, registered names, trademarks, service marks, etc. in this publication does not imply, even in the absence of a specific statement, that such names are exempt from the relevant protective laws and regulations and therefore free for general use.
The publisher, the authors and the editors are safe to assume that the advice and information in this book are believed to be true and accurate at the date of publication. Neither the publisher nor the authors or the editors give a warranty, express or implied, with respect to the material contained herein or for any errors or omissions that may have been made. The publisher remains neutral with regard to jurisdictional claims in published maps and institutional affiliations.

This Palgrave Pivot imprint is published by the registered company Springer Nature Switzerland AG.
The registered company address is: Gewerbestrasse 11, 6330 Cham, Switzerland

*There are two kinds of intelligence: one acquired,
As a child in school memorizes facts and concepts
With such intelligence you rise in the world.
There is another kind of tablet, one
Already completed and preserved inside you.
This other intelligence does not turn yellow or stagnate.
It's fluid, and it doesn't move from outside to inside
Through the conduits of plumbing-learning.
This second knowing is a fountainhead
From within you, moving out.*
Jalāl ad-Dīn Muhammad *Rūmī*

For Imaan

Foreword

It would be fair to say that recent years have witnessed an increase in attention to the role and nature of emotions as a core and necessary part of politics more generally and democratic education more specifically. This said, the need remains to conceptualise political emotions further, including how they are and might be operationalised within educational curricula and programmes in different contexts. Indeed, any worthwhile contribution to understanding this turn to the affective—what some (see Fortier 2010; Hung 2010) have called 'affective citizenship'—requires a careful unpicking and elucidation of the relevant philosophical, theological, sociological and educational perspectives at play.

To this end, in *Democratic Education and Muslim Philosophy: Understanding the Claims of Emotion*, Yusef Waghid and Nuraan Davids offer a sophisticated yet remarkably clear and accessible analysis of how and why democratic education can, does and should extend beyond reason and reasonableness to embrace intuition, experiences and emotions. The book is, in short, a highly timely and welcome contribution to the field. In drawing on and aligning concepts from the Western tradition and from the Islamic faith, the arguments and positions offered by the authors are insightful yet delicately nuanced. While there is no space in this Foreword to pay due attention (nor to give due credit) to all the arguments offered in the book, perhaps I can highlight briefly a few aspects of particular note that I think readers will find illuminating.

The exploration and clarification of gratitude offered in the book are excellent. As Cicero extolled, "gratitude is not only the greatest of virtues, but the parent of all others". And, yet, through particular interpretations and instantiations, gratitude has been criticised for a more negative form akin to something like obliged indebtedness. The analysis of gratitude offered in this book, particularly that found in Chap. 3, offers some highly pertinent reflections on how gratitude might be understood and approached as an 'act of emotion'. I was particularly struck by the suggestion that gratitude is a form of trust without contract and that, as educators in higher education, we should focus less on whether students show gratitude for our work and more on what the other (the student, in this case) has done for us. Of course, and as is duly noted in the book, the current conditions and cultures within higher education often act to constrain this form of gratitude. Many acts between students and academic staff, for example, are rendered and (re)constituted into the transactional. Nevertheless, returning ourselves to a humane and democratic form of gratitude offers exciting possibilities for teaching and learning, not least in recognising the other.

The practical examples and tensions expertly examined throughout the book remind us that teaching and engagement in higher education are first and foremost relational endeavours, but also that the relational can be risky and problematic. In this regard, the vignettes offered illuminate the rich tapestry of academic life in universities today, including its challenges and possibilities. Through their analyses, however, Waghid and Davids subtly tease out how the conceptual ideas they set out can help us to reflect on our relational interactions with students, colleagues and with wider institutions. It is only through thoughtful and reflective engagement with the emotional aspects of relationships and democratic education that we can fully understand them and, possibly, learn productive ways to respond to others.

The coda skilfully brings together the main themes and arguments of the book. More than this, the coda positions democratic education as an act in service of God (an act of *ibadah*) in the sense that democratic education cultivates humanity. One of the ways in democratic education cultivates humanity, of course, is through offering opportunities for genuinely deliberative encounters through which participants offer their interests, ideas and perspectives—including their emotions—in good faith. While not unrepresented in the current literature, the idea that democratic education involves service to others has become misdirected in recent years at the hands of some well-intentioned but misjudged attempts (albeit quite rightly) to challenge inequitable relationships between humans. Others would do well to read the sensitive consideration of service from the

Islamic perspective developed here. In particular, and by focusing on cultivating humanity, Waghid and Davids offer a perceptive reading of acting with justice in respect of others.

There is a gentleness to the positions and perspectives offered in the book that I find both attractive and compelling. My own view is that philosophy of education is best understood and approached as taking part in an ongoing conversation in which perspectives and ideas are presented and justified in the spirit of deliberation and reflection. This tack is taken by Waghid and Davids, too. As they conclude in the final page of the book, their endeavour is underpinned by the commitment to bring different traditions of thought and practice together "in conversation with each other". Certainly, through engaging with the contents of this book, readers will be invited and warmly welcomed into such a conversation. I hope it is one in which they will take part in the same spirit.

University of Birmingham Andrew Peterson
Birmingham, UK

References

Fortier, A.M. 2010. Proximity by Design? Affective Citizenship and the Management of Unease. *Citizenship Studies* 14 (1): 17–30.

Hung, R. 2010. In Search of Affective Citizenship: From the Pragmatist-Phenomenological Perspective. *Policy Futures in Education* 8 (5): 488–498.

Preface

Since Amy Gutmann's landmark publication entitled *Democratic Education* in 1987, much has been written about the subject in relation to human practices, such as pedagogy, management, leadership and institutional governance. At the core of the plethora of literature on democratic education over the last three decades, has been the overwhelming centrality of reason and its multifarious forms: rationality, reasonableness and justification. Not many, if any, of the most acclaimed contributions in and about the theoretical and practical understandings of democratic education have been audacious enough to foreground the significance of emotions in the cultivation of democratic education. Undeniably, the veracity of reason has made an indelible mark on the potentiality of democratic education to enact change in human relations. And, often reason has been considered the most significant 'truth' in the realisation of democratic education. Our analytical position in this book is that in addition to reason, there are other truths, which at first might not be as explicitly identifiable as reason. In this regard, our central focus shifts onto emotion, and we depart from the premise that perhaps emotion has been and is just as important as reason—if not more so. In examining the seminal ideas from prominent theorists on the subject of democratic education, we consider emotion as both an embodiment and enhancement of democratic education. To this end, we will look at the emotions of compassion, love, mercy, care, forgiveness, patience, gratitude, belligerence and empathy in relation to particular enactments and manifestations of democratic education.

What distinguishes this book from other books on democratic education is its willingness to depart from the languages constitutive of reason and reasonableness. Instead, the book seeks to understand that which seems to have manifested in reasonable pedagogical discourses to the extent that pre-eminence has altered the poise of reason in various forms of democratic education. The book is driven by a recognition that who the teacher is, whom he or she teaches, what he or she brings into the teaching-learning encounter, what is taught and how learning unfolds can neither be tied to reason only nor be constrained by it. There are other notions, intuitions, experiences (perceived and real)—particular emotions— at play, which yield to how democratic education is both conceptualised and embodied—no more so than in the moments of teaching and learning.

That democratic education involves people (teachers and students) implies particular contexts of discussion, deliberations, agreements and disagreements. Within these convergences of engagements are complexities of individuals and communities, which are always experienced through the senses. A teacher, for example, evokes or provokes particular feelings and emotions before the teaching even commences, which, in turn, speaks to the student's eagerness or reluctance to participate in his or her own learning. A student's ability to discern between good and bad teaching, at times, pertains to a teacher's preparedness, content knowledge and/or pedagogical practices. At other times, whether or not a student finds enjoyment from a particular class has very little to do with what is being taught, but rather with who is doing the teaching—that is, how a teacher makes the student feel. How a student feels has some (if not, significant) effects on his or her learning. This same is true for teachers in relation to teaching and how they experience students. A teacher who is disinterested in and disconnected from his or her teaching cannot expect that students would find the lessons interesting; they will experience a teacher as he or she presents him- or herself. Emotions, therefore, are profoundly present in how democratic education is experienced. Conceptions of respect, tolerance and compassion are empty if they are not made visible within pedagogy, and hence, warrant explication and illustration.

In Chap. 1, we examine the seminal thoughts of Amy Gutmann (1987, 2003) in relation to emotions. More specifically, we show how freedom is enhanced by emotions. Chapter 2, in reference to the thoughts of Seyla Benhabib (1996, 2011), shows how deliberative iterations are guided by emotions. Chapter 3 explores Jacques Derrida's notion of democratic education in relation to gratitude. Chapter 4 looks at the notions of belligerence and distress in the works of Eamonn Callan (1997) in relation to emotions. In Chap. 5, we revisit Martha Nussbaum's notion of compassionate action and show how such an emotive judgement seems to underscore and guide democratic education. Chapter 6 explores Syed Muhammad Naquib al-Attas's idea of *ta'dib* (good education) and shows how the emotive idea of *adab* (goodness) can engender more plausible democratic actions. Chapter 7 elucidates Ibn al-Arabi's idea of human freedom and how it affects democratic human relations. In Chap. 8, we show how Ibn Sina's idea of intuition may be considered an emotive action that could cultivate democratic educational experiences. Chapter 9 examines Fazlur Rahman's analysis of *shura* (consultation) and its ramifications for democratic education in relation to the emotions. In Chap. 10, we reflect on Muhammad Iqbal's conception of *ijtihad* (exertion) and its implications for democratic education.

Of course, we have not avoided the theme of emotions in our writings. More recently, we have written about the emotion of a pedagogic pilgrimage, nuances of care and even university freedom. However, what makes this contribution unique is that our consideration of theoretical ideas as articulated above emanates from a distinctive position of bearing witness to emotions ourselves and then set out to show how the emotions manifest in pedagogic practices and, concomitantly, in the theoretical ideas of leading scholars in the field of philosophy of education. Put differently, this book represents our engagement with emotions and at the same time attempts to make sense of these engagements in relation to the theoretical works of leading scholars. The point is, as rational and emotive beings, we offer and give account of our experiences of being rational and emotive in relation to existing theories on emotions and education.

What makes this book distinctive and perhaps expansive in thought and practice is that we recognise the significance of bringing leading theorists on democratic education in the contemporary world of philosophy of education into direct conversation with an understanding of Muslim scholarship. We recognise not only the phenomenal contributions scholars in the Western world have to offer in terms of the cultivation of the notion of democratic education and the claims of emotion they make, but also how leading Muslim scholars proffer ways according to which democratic education can be enacted. This is so, despite the fact that democratic education is looked upon spuriously in several Muslim-dominated countries and circles, especially in many political autocracies in the Middle East.

We have attempted to offer here an enriched and expansive notion of democratic education that can be situated in what can be conceived of as both rational and emotional. Democratic education would not exist if incommensurate with a justification of reasons. And, making judgements in defence of various truth claims—especially about the human condition—does not happen without invoking the emotions, in other words, devoid of sentiment and soul. It is here that we found views of Western and non-Western, most notably Muslim, theorists in the pursuit of democratic education quite complementary and thoughtful. Of course, rationality and emotion are not separate entities, as one cannot assume to offer a rational judgement without fervour. Likewise, an emotive response does not have to be irrational, as arguing passionately for truth claims does not necessarily occur without reasons and justifications. In our view, rationality and emotion exist on a continuum to the extent that at times, one's argument, for instance, can be less provocative, (and, by implication, emotive) whereas, at other times, arguments can be highly emotive without being irrational. The theorists we chose and on whose enunciations in and about democratic education we expound can be considered rational-cum-emotive. Equally, our choice of Western and non-Western, in particular Muslim, scholars is informed by an understanding that elucidations of democratic education can be richly expanded beyond notions of liberality.

Stellenbosch, South Africa   Nuraan Davids
                                                              Yusef Waghid

References

Benhabib, S. (Ed.). 1996. *Democracy and Difference: Contesting the Boundaries of the Political*. Princeton, NJ: Princeton University Press.
Benhabib, S. 2011. *Dignity in Adversity: Human Rights in Troubled Times*. Cambridge: Polity Press.
Callan, E. 1997. *Creating Citizens: Political Education and Liberal Democracy*. Oxford: Oxford University Press.
Gutmann, A. 1987. *Democratic Education*. Princeton, NJ: Princeton University Press.
———. 2003. *Identity in Democracy*. Princeton and Oxford: Princeton University Press.

Contents

1. Democratic Education and Deliberative Freedom: A Defence of Co-learning ... 1

2. Democratic Education and Iterations: On the Emotion of Talking Back ... 15

3. Democratic Education and Gratitude ... 27

4. Belligerence and Distress as Emotions in Democratic Education ... 39

5. Democratic Education and Compassion ... 49

6. *Adab* and Democratic Education ... 61

7. Ibn al-Arabi's Idea of *Al-insan Al-kamil* (the Perfect Human) and Democratic Education ... 71

8. Ibn Sina's Notion of Intuition and Claims of Democratic Education ... 81

9 Fazlur Rahman's Notion of *Shura* and Its Implications
   for Democratic Education   91

10 Muhammad Iqbal's Conception of *Ijtihad* and Its
   Implications for Democratic Education   99

Coda: Democratic Education as an Act of *Ibadah*   109

Index   115

About the Authors

Nuraan Davids is Professor of Philosophy of Education in the Faculty of Education at Stellenbosch University, South Africa. Her most recent co-authored books with Yusef Waghid are *Universities, Pedagogical Encounters, Openness, and Free Speech: Reconfiguring Democratic Education* (2019) and *Teaching and Learning as a Pedagogic Pilgrimage: Cultivating Faith, Hope and Imagination* (2019).

Yusef Waghid is Distinguished Professor of Philosophy of Education at Stellenbosch University, South Africa. He is the author of *Towards a Philosophy of Caring in Higher Education: Pedagogy and Nuances of Care* (Palgrave Macmillan 2019); co-author (with Nuraan Davids) of *Universities, Pedagogical Encounters, Openness, and Free Speech: Reconfiguring Democratic Education* (2019); and co-editor (with Manthalu Herbert Chikumbutso) of *Decolonisation and Decoloniality of Education in Africa* (Palgrave Macmillan 2019).

CHAPTER 1

Democratic Education and Deliberative Freedom: A Defence of Co-learning

Abstract In this chapter, we offer an account of Berlin's (*Four Essays on Liberty*, Oxford University Press, 1969) conceptions of positive and negative liberty. We bring into contestation the argument that an individual's freedom to act autonomously, without any interference or constraint, can ever be the case, if one considers, that an individual's action is always in relation to others, and hence, always conditional. We draw on Gutmann's (*Democratic Education*, Princeton University Press, 1987) argument that an individual's freedom does not happen independently from the exercise of freedom by others which, in turn, constrains their freedom as they do things in collaboration with others. Consequently, the exercise of freedom is both autonomous and interdependent: autonomous freedom is exercised through individual human agency; and interdependent human freedom is practised in relation with others. We contend that at the heart democratic education is the notion of deliberative freedom: to act with deliberative rationality, and to pursue one's engagement with others on the basis of an emotive freedom, that enhances the possibility for co-learning and ethical judgement of a rational and emotive kind.

Keywords Positive liberty • Negative liberty • Autonomy • Deliberative freedom

Introduction

On reading Amy Gutmann's (1987) *Democratic Education* again, we are confronted by the way in which the emotion of freedom comes up as a precondition for human engagement. Being unfree and constrained can never be a defence for plausible human actions as humans are meant to be free in the first place. Humans are free in the sense that they can think and make choices, whether in relation to where they live, what they eat or whom they choose to marry or where to work. Within an educational setting, humans can choose where they wish to study, what they wish to pursue, what to read and, if they continue in the academic realm, in which discipline they wish to specialise. They are free because they do not merely decide in advance which knowledge interests they endeavour to pursue, but also how they wish to do it. Their choices and procedures to embark on educational research, for instance, are corroborated and enhanced by the capacities to exercise their freedoms. In this way, humans are unique and their freedoms are unconstrained.

Yet, as reminded by Gutmann (1987), to enact one's freedom does not happen independently from the exercise of freedom by others, which in turn constrains their freedom as they do things in collaboration with others. Individuals might not always agree with each other but momentarily seek agreement for the sake of formulating a point of view, and, at a later stage, might even be persuaded by the very idea or understanding with which they might have been troubled previously. Consequently, their exercise of freedom is both autonomous and interdependent: autonomous freedom is exercised through individual human agency; and interdependent human freedom is practised in relation with others. Interdependence with others somewhat inhibits individuals' freedom, especially if they initially needed to be persuaded. But, their intersubjective agreement does not imply that, as a collective, they are now constrained. As we co-author this book, we are both provoked by our independence of thought as autonomous humans; concurrently, we are also informed by one another's understandings as we collectively embark on shaping our thoughts in union for the purposes of producing a lucid and coherent argument in the book. In short, we remain autonomously and collectively unconstrained. This brings us to a discussion of autonomous freedom and deliberative freedom.

From Autonomous Freedom to Deliberative Freedom

In this section, we do not want to expound further on the distinction Isaiah Berlin makes between positive and negative freedom as such analyses are replete in the literature in and about philosophy and philosophy of education. Suffice to say that Berlin (1969) identifies positive freedom as freedom exercised autonomously by the individual—a way of acting with self-determination to realise his or her aspirations, unhindered by the freedom of others. Negative freedom on the other hand is freedom which, when exercised, negates the freedoms of others as it considers the exercise of freedom in the absence of interference by others. In sum, while positive freedom or liberty is a form of autonomous action whereby an individual exerts him- or herself in the pursuit of independent judgements, negative freedom is a form of autonomous action unhindered by external constraints.

Autonomous freedom in the way we shall expound seems to resonate with an understanding of positive freedom. And, perhaps it does, as the exercise of individual liberty is at stake in both positive and autonomous freedoms. However, our elucidation of this concept of autonomous freedom relates to the exercise of individual freedom unconstrained by the interference of others. In Berlin's explication of positive freedom, there is a possibility for others to encroach on the individual freedoms of people. In other words, individuals exercise their freedom, but not necessarily unconstrained by the acts of others. Autonomous freedom, we hold, is a freedom exercised by individuals unhampered by the freedom of others. Thus, when individuals exercise their freedom to leave their country of origin for the purposes of making their life elsewhere, or when a student disagrees with a teacher, they exercise individual freedoms. This is so on the basis that their freedoms are unhampered by the freedom of others. In other words, migrants leave their country of origin irrespective of the impingement of others to prevent them from doing so. Or, a student challenges a teacher on his or her views, without being constrained by the teacher to do so. If the latter happens, unlike positive freedom, unconstrained human action ensues. Such a view of autonomous freedom offers a different dimension to democratic education in the sense that such a form of education cannot exist if the individual freedoms of people are curtailed or encroached upon by others. Positive freedom happens with the possibility that one's individual liberty can be constrained even in the wake of exercising one's self-determination in the realisation of one's aspirations.

Of course, the question can be asked whether autonomous freedom is at all possible and whether it is not possible for others to leave one's freedom to one's self. It might be that the possibility exists for others to interrupt an individual's exercise of his or her autonomous freedom, but this is not what happens when autonomous action becomes manifest. It could be argued, for example, that the perceived freedom of a migrant to leave his or her home was, in fact, not motivated by an autonomous freedom, but rather by particular conditions of strife, threat or hunger, which forced the migrant to make that decision. But, then, of course, the argument stands that the migrant still exercised his or her freedom to stay or leave and was neither forced to stay nor forced to leave. Autonomous action is, therefore, only possible if others constrain the exercise of their individual freedoms. And, the latter in itself brings into consideration the idea that autonomous freedom per se is an impossibility, as it requires of others to limit their freedoms. This makes autonomous freedom an exercise of conditionality as it happens only when others restrain their actions or exercise freedom. It would seem that even within perceived acts of autonomous action, such as deciding to migrate, are affected by particular conditions or constraints, which might at first not be evident, these conditions are present, nevertheless. We are confronted, therefore, with the idea of an unconstrained or autonomous freedom, which might in itself be a misnomer because while individuals possess the capacity to take autonomous actions, individuals exist within particular contexts and conditions, which cannot be discounted from whatever action is taken. Considering that autonomous freedom is not in its entirety possible, as the freedoms of others would always be there to interrupt what seems to be autonomous, we now turn to a discussion of deliberative freedom.

What we have been doing thus far is to show that the exercise of autonomous freedom in its entirety might not be possible as there are limits to what an individual does or can do. For example, a teacher might claim that he or she is a deeply religious person whose life, in all respects, is lived in relation to the doctrines of that particular religion. He or she might wish to take this affinity into his or her classroom and his or her teaching—possibly through adopting certain practices in relation to discipline, or refusing to discuss certain topics, for example. A teacher might assert that since his or her religious identity is constitutive of his or her professional identity as a teacher, he or she should not be expected to discount that characteristic of him- or herself and that he or she is exercising his or her individual right to express him- or herself as such. He or she might also insist that he or she be respected for his or her particular religious views and identity and that others should not interfere in his or her right to do so—since this is his or her religious freedom. However, the mere expectation that others should not interfere with such teacher's right to assert his or her religious identity in his or her class is an expectation of non-interference, and hence, an infringement or constraint on others *not* to act. The scenario, which unfolds is one, which makes the teacher's right to exercise his or her religious freedom conditionally upon the non-interference of others. And, if such a conditionality manifests, the teacher's autonomous freedom can no longer be an independent one unhampered by what others do. In this instance, a teacher's autonomous freedom to express his or her religious views seems to be dependent upon the will of others not to interfere. Considering that autonomous freedom is dependent on the conditionality that others should not interfere, freedom can no longer be autonomous, as autonomy in itself demands the non-interference of others, who, in this case, seem to exercise an interference of passivity. That is, they do not interfere; yet, they do so passively or inadvertently. Now, if an understanding of autonomous freedom is not possible, which kind of freedom is possible?

For us, the exercise of freedom is not an act of singularity whereby an individual simply does as he or she pleases, or says what he or she wants to say. The exercise of freedom is a dialectical practice as one cannot be free or act freely without at least the presence of others. Stated differently, when an individual acts or says something, it is in response to a particular context or others. In the case of the example above, the teacher wants to insert his or her religious identity into his or her teaching. He or she also expects non-interference from others. Yet, others cannot be excluded from his or her action. Of course, a physical presence is not always a requirement. For instance, when an academic exercises his or her freedom to write on a particular topic or theme, he or she invariably considers the views of others who might have written on the topic or theme previously—that is, he or she takes into account existing views on the topic. These views might lead him or her to reconsider the views that he or she had intended to write when he or she initially thought about the topic. Or, he or she might feel even more emboldened about his or her initial ideas, after reading the existing debates on the topic. The point is that the presence of people and their views does not necessarily have to be physical. Even the virtual presence of others, or their ideas, could constrain the freedom of individuals. This brings us to our argument in defence of deliberative freedom. Berlin's (1969) idea of negative freedom, unconstrained by the freedom of others, does not seem to be possible. It is not possible to exercise one's individual liberty unhampered implicitly or explicitly from the freedoms of others. Simply put, it does not make sense to talk about a freedom exercised in isolation unrestricted by the views of others. Consequently, the idea of autonomous freedom seems to be an impossibility. However, what seems to be a possibility is a kind of deliberative freedom whereby humans exercise their freedoms in an encumbered way—that is, their freedoms are constrained by the presence of others' freedom. We want to make a case for deliberative freedom as a way to move beyond an exclusively autonomous freedom.

In the first instance, deliberative freedom takes into account the rational freedoms of others. An individual might exercise his or her freedom unhampered by what he or she might have thought to be the freedom of others, which Berlin (1969) couches through his idea of negative freedom, but he or she does not really do so. The exercise of individual freedom, according to Gutmann (2003), is an important part of democratic justice, and is, therefore, conditional upon the freedoms of others. Gutmann believes that in a democratic society, individuals are free to associate with whomever they please. They are free to join groups, including identity groups based on religion, race and ethnicity, gender and sexual orientation, partisan politics and national origin. Similar identity groups emerge in classrooms and schools—confirming that identity politics are as evident in educational settings as they are elsewhere.

Gutmann (2003) argues that freedom, if unjust, cannot be left unconstrained. That is, all freedoms are conditional upon this or that—more specifically, all human freedoms are conditional upon what individuals do in or out of the presence of others. Gutmann (2003) contends that, as soon as injustice to others unfolds, freedom can no longer be left unconstrained. However, argues Gutmann (2003), the right to free association ends where injustice to others begins. As we write this chapter, we are reminded of a recent event in which a number of students protested against a lecturer using Afrikaans as a language of instruction—a language, which a number of students are unable to understand, and a language, which for many South Africans is associated with the painful legacy of apartheid. What started as a disagreement on the issue of language, quickly escalated into a conflict on identity politics and created a clear line between groups, between those who were in support of Afrikaans and those who were not. On the one hand, a lecturer claimed her right to speak in her mother tongue. On the other hand, a number of students felt marginalised and excluded, because of the right being exercised by the lecturer. Gutmann in an interview with Sardoc (2018, 248) argues that we must not lose sight of the role of educators themselves, citizens whose religious, political and social commitments have already been shaped, even if not fully formed. She remarks, "[t]o remain vibrant and productive, democracies rely on a loop that begins not only with the young people who are to be taught, but with the adults who will teach them" (Sardoc 2018, 248).

Following Gutmann (2003), the actions of the lecturer have to be constrained, since her actions had resulted in an injustice towards the students, who could not understand her, or who felt affronted about being taught in a language, which they associate with the oppression of apartheid. Both groups—those in support and those in opposition—had valid justifications for their positions. What is necessary, according to Gutmann (2003) to resolve this impasse, is to bridge the divide of identity politics through processes of deliberation. In her interview with Sardoc (2018, 249), Gutmann remarked:

> A free people have multiple identities that are open to alterable interpretations based upon our socialization, education, and deliberations over time with many others. When it comes to making democratic decisions, no more effective or respectful means has yet to be found for imperfect individuals to make the most just decisions possible than deliberation that is iterative over time.

In agreement with Gutmann (2003), we contend that freedom is conditional upon the justifications proffered in defence of freedoms, and the latter implies that freedom is never really autonomous; it is exercised in conjunction with the justifications others proffer in defence of their freedoms. This in itself makes freedom highly engaging, that is to say, deliberative. The point is that autonomous freedom is constituted within deliberative freedom. Put differently, what makes deliberative freedom what it is, is that individual freedoms are exercised co-dependently. One's freedom is therefore conditional upon the exercise of others' freedoms and both freedoms—of oneself and of others—are then exercised co-dependently. We shall now address the claim that deliberative freedom is constituted by individual or autonomous freedoms.

On What Constitutes Deliberative Freedom

By now, it seems evident that deliberative freedom as a freedom exercised co-dependently can neither be exclusively positive (because self-determination cannot really happen unconstrained by the freedom of others) nor exclusively negative (as an individual's exercise of freedom cannot really happen unconstrained in the absence of others and their freedoms). Therefore, our analysis of freedom is not one of being positive or negative; rather, it shows how freedom manifests in deliberation with others. Firstly, when humans exercise their freedom in relation with one another, they do so in recognition of one another's presence—whether physical or not. This means that when reading a text, a person exercises his or her freedom to construct, reconstruct and deconstruct meanings as if the other person—who might be the author of such a text—is in the presence of the person doing the reading. Such a person's (re)constructions or deconstructions occur as if the other is always there—whether physically or virtually—and often, the sense the reader makes of a text is conditional upon what he or she finds to be in the text or what the text reveals. For instance, reading a book cannot simply be about an utterance of words and thoughts of someone else (or one's own, if one is the author of the book). Rather, what one reads and makes sense of, depends on one's interpretation of what is read. The interpretation of the text hinges on whatever lived experiences and context are brought to the reading. This is why readings yield different meanings and emotions to different readers. Of course, this erasure or "death of the author" is most famously captured by Roland Barthes (1988, 6) as follows:

> In this way is revealed the whole being of writing: a text consists of multiple writings, issuing from several cultures and entering into dialogue with each other, into parody, into contestation; but there is one place where this multiplicity is collected, united, and this place is not the author, as we have hitherto said it was, but the reader: the reader is the very space in which are inscribed, without any being lost, all the citations a writing consists of; the unity of a text is not in its origin, it is in its destination; but this destination can no longer be personal: the reader is a man without history, without biography, without psychology; he is only that someone who holds gathered into a single field all the paths of which the text is constituted.

When one reads, one is able to make certain inferences and judgements on account of what is read. One might read as if the author of the book is in one's presence, so one might take into account what the author had written previously. When this happens, one makes sense of a text as if the author of the text speaks to one—that is, constructs, reconstructs and deconstructs meanings. Put differently, when reading and interpreting, one freely offers one's understanding and judgement of what is being read, in other words, one interprets a text in a particular way.

Yet, as time passes and one reads the text again, the text might be interpreted differently, with new connotations and experiences. The author, therefore, is understood differently—because one brings a different set of deliberations to the text. One comes with renewed understandings, questions and expectations of engagement, which might have been present during the initial reading. Hence, when one exercises such a freedom where one imagines an author to talk back to one and then, one in turn, offers a different judgement, one can be said to articulate one's judgements in a deliberative way. Put differently, one would then have engaged with a text with a kind of deliberative freedom. The practice of democratic deliberation, explains Rostbøll (2008, 3), "is dialectically interrelated with multiple dimensions of freedom". These different dimensions of freedom, he continues, are what make actual deliberation possible. Concomitantly, democratic deliberation is needed in order to understand, justify and realise the different dimensions of freedom, according to Rostbøll (2008). Hence, the relationship between deliberative democracy and the different dimensions of freedom "is dialectical and coconstitutive. It is a relationship of mutual justification and reciprocal reinforcement" (Rostbøll 2008).

Deliberative freedom therefore happens when one and another co-exist and the meanings constructed by one happen as a corollary of being co-dependent on the meanings that emanate from both parties—that is, oneself and the other. Likewise, a university student does not just learn from a teacher. A teacher might introduce ideas or texts to a student, but meanings that ensue on account of both a student and teacher happen as a result of the teacher and student making sense of one another's pronouncements. For this reason, learning is not necessarily dependent on teaching. In other words, a student does not have to be told what to think and how to think, in order for learning to unfold. Learning happens when a learner makes meaning or sense of a particular topic or analysis. Similarly, a teacher cannot assume that teaching has occurred by virtue of the fact that he or she had stepped into a classroom and had taught on this or that topic. Teaching only occurs when learning unfolds. The two practices—teaching and learning—therefore exist in a dyadic relationship, where the one relies on and derives from the other. In a different way, both teacher and student are co-learners. The teacher has to learn how to engage and deliberate with his or her learners. He or she has to figure out a way of making his or her teaching accessible to his or her students. Learning happens when both teacher and student make sense of that to which they are exposed and, in some way, when they are informed by one another's understandings, co-learning ensues. The upshot of this argument is that co-learning is inextricably linked to co-dependence on meanings being derived and deliberated on as a result of exercising one's freedom as a teacher in deliberation with a student. Deliberative freedom hence gives rise to co-dependence and co-learning.

When one co-learns in a deliberative space, one does not do so only on the basis of agreement and dissensus on what counts as reasonable and defensible, but also on account of how one and others become emotionally attuned to what has been co-learned. To Gutmann (in interview with Sardoc 2018, 246), deliberative democracy creates the spaces for an ongoing process of mutual justification, which is based on mutual respect. One can be persuaded by reasons but this does not mean that one learns only through a deliberative intellectual exchange of thoughts. Often, one is also directed by one's intuitiveness as to whether something is persuasive or not. In such a situation, one's learning is both connected to the intellectual (on account of being persuaded or dissuaded by reasons) and the emotional (on the basis that one is also initiated in a formation of meaning making through intuitive endeavours). Co-learning can then be considered being a result of people's intellectual and emotional pursuits of ideas. Next, we examine the implication of co-learning and co-dependence for democratic education.

Co-learning, Co-dependence and Democratic Education

Thus far, we have construed an argument in defence of co-learning on the basis of exercising deliberative freedom. If one considers that democratic education involves the engagement of people in some kind of intellectual (and emotional, we would assert) activity of meaning making, then such an understanding of democratic education invokes understandings of, say, teachers and students, in a co-dependent way. In this sense, the pursuit of democratic education is tantamount to a co-dependent engagement of human activity. In other words, democratic education cannot manifest without human co-dependence and engagement of matters that concern humans. To forge and support beneficial compromises in decision-making, and a basic understanding of the value of deliberation—as well as its limits—all are keys to improving pluralist democratic societies. For this reason, Gutmann (in Sardoc 2018, 248) contends that, foremost among the skills and virtues necessary for conscious social reproduction is not mindless replication, but rather mindful change over time, brought forth through deliberation. The mere fact that humans are co-dependent in their engagement implies that their learning is collaborative: they listen attentively to one another, make sense of one another's points of view, take into critical scrutiny of one another's perspectives and learn in a collaborative fashion. Co-dependent learning is inextricably connected to the notion of democratic engagement. By implication, democratic education cannot unfold in human relations without a recognition of co-learning and co-dependence.

Co-learning allows academics in a university, for example, to act with deliberative freedom to make judgements—even of an ethical kind—about their specific inquiry. In a way, co-learning therefore invokes the freedom of scholars in a university "to assess existing theories, established institutions, and widely held beliefs according to the canons of truth adopted by their academic disciplines without fear of sanction by anyone if they arrive at unpopular conclusions" (Gutmann 1987, 175).

The point about reaching unpopular conclusions during intellectual inquiry has to do with academic freedom, which scholars pursue without fear of any form of reprisal in making ethical judgements—a matter of invoking emotivism as well as rationality. In other words, the exercise of academic freedom through collaboration and deliberation is a highly emotive exercise in the pursuit of intellectual inquiry. It is for this reason that we concur with Gutmann (1987, 176) who avers that democratic education obliges people "not to restrict the intellectual freedom of individual scholars or those freedoms of liberal universities that secure an institutional environment conducive to the exercise of scholarly autonomy". The point about democratic education constituted by deliberative freedom in a university, provides what Gutmann (1987, 179) refers to as "an institutional sanctuary against repression, which prevents majorities or coalitions of minorities from controlling the creation of politically relevant ideas". In this way, democratic education with both a rational and emotive intent can secure the freedom of scholars to speak out and or prevent, for instance, racially and sexually discriminatory promotion practices (Gutmann 1987, 179). When joined together in a robust and respectful learning environment

> [S]tudents who represent a rich diversity of religions and socioeconomic backgrounds, cultural and political orientations, races and ethnicities, and genders and sexualities help to facilitate better understanding and better ideas for improving their own individual lives and the lives of our societies and our world. (Gutmann in interview with Sardoc 2018, 250)

It is a democratic education underscored by deliberative freedom that makes co-learning and engagement among people possible—those who can, for example, defend universities against autonomous state regulation and other discriminatory practices.

Summary

We commenced this chapter by deliberating on Berlin's (1969) conceptions of positive and negative liberty. We brought into contestation the argument that an individual's freedom to act autonomously, without any interference or constraint, can never be the case, if one considers that an individual's action is always in relation to others and, hence, always conditional. We drew on Gutmann's (1987) argument that an individual's freedom does not happen independently from the exercise of freedom by others which, in turn, constrains an individual's freedom as they do things in collaboration with others. Consequently, the exercise of freedom is both autonomous and interdependent: autonomous freedom is exercised through individual human agency, and interdependent human freedom is practised in relation with others. Consequently, we argued that, at the heart democratic education is the notion of deliberative freedom to act with deliberative rationality and to pursue one's engagement with others on the basis of an emotive freedom. When such a form of democratic education is pursued, the possibility for co-learning and ethical judgement of a rational and emotive kind would invariably ensue. In the next chapter, we consider how deliberative iterations guide the emotion of talking back in and through democratic education.

REFERENCES

Barthes, R. 1988. The Death of the Author. In *Modern Criticism and Theory*, ed. D. Lodge, 166–195. Harlow: Longman House.
Berlin, I. 1969. Two Concepts of Liberty. In *Four Essays on Liberty*, ed. I. Berlin, 118–172. London: Oxford University Press.
Gutmann, A. 1987. *Democratic Education*. Princeton, NJ: Princeton University Press.
———. 2003. *Identity in Democracy*. Princeton, NJ: Princeton University Press.
Rostbøll, C.F. 2008. *Deliberative Freedom: Deliberative Democracy as Critical Theory*. Albany, NY: University of New York Press.
Sardoc, M. 2018. Democratic Education at 30: An Interview with Dr Amy Gutmann. *Theory and Research in Education* 16 (2): 244–252.

CHAPTER 2

Democratic Education and Iterations: On the Emotion of Talking Back

Abstract In this chapter, we focus on Benhabib's (*The Rights of Others: Aliens, Residents and Citizens*, Cambridge University Press, 2004) conception of democratic iteration, as being at the core of democratic education. We posit that the premise of democratic iterations is not to alter the normative validity of practical discourses, but to determine the legitimacy of particular processes of opinion and will formation. In this regard, we focus on two examples: one commonly referred to as the French scarf affair and the other involving the prohibition of 'black languages and hair' in South African schools. We argue that it would be unjustifiable to delink democratic education from rational articulations and rearticulations and emotional will formation.

Keywords Democratic iteration • Practice • Rational articulation • Will formation

INTRODUCTION

Schools, as we know, are incredibly dynamic spaces—exemplified by numerous and complex intersections of identities—of teachers, learners, parents and communities. With the immense diversity implicit and explicit in constructions of race, religion, culture, ethnicity, language, class and sexuality, the chances of disagreement and controversy are inevitable.

© The Author(s) 2019
N. Davids, Y. Waghid, *Democratic Education and Muslim Philosophy*, https://doi.org/10.1007/978-3-030-30056-2_2

Some, like Mouffe (2000), would describe these conflicts and controversies as a necessary part of a democracy. While not particularly unusual, therefore, South African schools continue to face disturbing challenges in relation to racism, discrimination and exclusion since desegregating about 25 years ago. At times, these dehumanising practices present themselves in different ways through odd, yet taken-for-granted institutional regulations and prescriptions pertaining to language—and even hair. More recently, for example, a number of historically advantaged (white) schools came into controversy for prohibiting black learners from speaking 'African languages' and insisting on the exclusive use of English. Another handful of schools had implemented hair regulations, which effectively forced black girls to straighten their "untidy afros chemically" (Pather 2016). Not surprisingly, learners responded in anger and frustration, bringing into contestation the imposition of "colonialist, white" (Pather 2016) norms, which continue to beset South African schools, despite the constitutional democracy. While the ensuing protests created tension and conflict at these schools, the protests opened the proverbial door to much-needed debate on the types of norms and traditions, into which all learners are expected to assimilate—often at a cost to their own self-identities and self-understandings.

From these conflicts, we learn that human engagement is not always smooth and untroubling. Sometimes, the engagement can be uneasy and provocative. But, for as long participants in an encounter are not remiss of the importance of dissensus and dissonance, the possibility is always there for such an encounter to be in becoming. In this chapter, we firstly consider why and how the practice of iteration can enhance human encounters. Secondly, we analyse how iteration augments the possibility of democratic education. Thirdly, we proffer reasons why iteration is an act of emotion and a way of deepening responsible human acts.

Cultivating Iterative Human Encounters

"Iteration", as Benhabib (2004, 14) clarifies, is a term which was introduced into the philosophy of language by Derrida (1988). In the process of repeating a term or a concept, explains Benhabib (2004, 14–15), "we never simply produce a replica of the original usage and its intended meaning: rather, every repetition is a form of variation. Every iteration transforms meaning, enriches it in ever-so-subtle ways." In fact, she contends, there really is no 'originary' source of meaning, or an 'original' to which all subsequent forms must conform. To Benhabib (2004, 15), iteration is the reappropriation of the 'origin'; it is at the same time its dissolution as the original and its preservation through its continuous deployment. Following on this understanding, she conceives of 'democratic iterations' as "linguistic, legal, cultural and political repetitions-in-transformation, invocations which are also revocations. They not only change established understandings but also transform what passes as the valid or established view of an authoritative precedent" (Benhabib 2004, 15). She proposes a model of democratic iterations through which the values of private and public autonomy can be rearticulated. For Benhabib (2004, 11, 17),

[Democratic iterations are] complex ways of mediating the will- and opinion-formation of democratic majorities with cosmopolitan norms [...] complex processes of public argument, deliberation and exchange through which universalist rights claims are contested and contextualized, invoked and revoked, posited and repositioned, throughout legal and political institutions, as well as in the associations of civil society.

Benhabib (2011, 151) offers three ways for thinking about democratic iterations: firstly, such human encounters centre on conversations and deliberations that can guarantee inclusivity and equality of participation. That is, in order for any deliberative encounter to be deemed legitimate, it should create opportunities for fairness and inclusiveness. By legitimacy, Benhabib (1996, 68) means that people should participate freely and engage unconstrainedly in public deliberation about matters that concern them. That is, "public sphere of deliberation of all about matters of mutual concern is essential to the legitimacy of democratic institutions" (Benhabib 1996, 68). Equality of participation implies that people use their sense of reason as moral and political equals to exercise judgements on "decisions affecting the well-being of a collectivity" (Benhabib 1996, 68). Put differently, "what is considered in the common interest of all results from processes of collective deliberation conducted rationally and fairly among free and equal individuals" (Benhabib 1996, 69). In this regard, democratic iterations attest to a dialectic of rights and identities. In such processes, she elaborates that, "both the identities involved and the very meaning of rights claims are reappropriated, resignified and imbued with new and different meaning" (Benhabib 2004, 24).

Secondly, democratic iterations are concerned with people's moral, political and constitutional commitments towards the achievement of democratic justice, as well as their international obligations to collective human rights treaties and texts (Benhabib 2011, 152). In other words, democratic iterations should be geared towards protecting people's basic rights and liberties without silencing dissent and curtailing minority views (Benhabib 1996, 77). Through democratic iterations, "norms of universal moral respect and egalitarian reciprocity allow minorities and dissenters both the right to withhold their assent and the right to challenge the rules … of public debate" (Benhabib 1996, 79). And, when people engage in democratic iterations, they focus on non-coercive and non-final processes of opinion formation in an unrestricted public sphere (Benhabib 1996, 76). In citing specific examples of public confrontations with an individual's rights to freedom of conscience and religion—as encountered in the French and German "scarf affairs", as well as the Turkish "turban affair", Benhabib (2011, 182) maintains that, through such controversies, the dialectic of rights and identities is mobilised in processes of democratic iterations.[1] Rights and other principles of the liberal democratic state, contends Benhabib (2011, 182), need to be challenged periodically and rearticulated in the public sphere in order to retain and enrich their original meaning.

Thirdly, democratic iterations involve processes of public self-reflection and public defensiveness that allow conclusions to be deliberated on and the possibility that others might reflect on such conclusions with the intention to challenge them through plausible reasons (Benhabib 1996, 72). In other words, iterations involve practices of examination, challenge, criticism and rearticulation. Simply put, deliberative rationality underscores iterations. As aptly put by Benhabib (1996, 72),

> [T]he equal chance of all affected to initiate such [iterative] discourse of deliberation suggests that no outcome is prima facie fixed but can be revised and subjected to reexamination … [that is] this conclusion can remain valid until challenged by good reasons [of reflection and defensiveness] by some other group.

To summarise briefly, democratic iterations happen in unconstrained public spheres on the basis of equal participation and inclusiveness in and

---

[1] Commonly referred to as a politico-cultural debate or conflict, the scarf affair has become a generic reference to the controversial decision by a number of European liberal democracies to regulate the dress code of Muslim women—specifically, to compel Muslim women not to wear their head scarves in the public sphere.

about matters that legitimately concern people. Iterations are morally and politically informed, and manifest on the basis of mutual respect, egalitarian reciprocity and dissent among participants. Moreover, iterations are geared towards the achievement of democratic justice guided by both public reflection and public defensiveness on the part of participants. Now that we have examined the notion of democratic iterations, we turn our attention to how such iterations connect with the emotions.

Democratic Iterations and the Emotions

From the aforementioned, it can be inferred that democratic iterations "involve complex processes of public argument, deliberation, and exchange through which universalist rights claims are contested and contextualised, invoked and revoked ... in the associations of civil society" (Benhabib 2011, 16). Argumentation, deliberation and rights claims do not just involve principles of rationality but also the emotive experiences of participants engaged in such iterations. Articulating and defending an argument do not just involve the justifications (in terms of words and sentences) people proffer. In addition, articulating and defending also involve an invocation of people's feelings vis-à-vis the responses they give on account of matters of public concern. Likewise, staking one's claims to rights is not just a rational one action, but also an emotional one.

In the way people communicate, they invariably use their intellect and senses as thoughts are emotive expressions of the human mind. In this regard, we concur with Benhabib (2011, 129) when she states, "[e]very iteration transforms meaning, adds to it, enriches it in ever so subtle [and emotive] ways". It is therefore unsurprising to find that Benhabib is adamant that iterations enable us to judge interpretations of rights claims and opinions of will formation that regulate our lives, in other words, a clear indication that claims are not just constituted in rational argumentation but also guided by the will of the emotions. As aptly stated by Benhabib (2011, 130), iterations about human rights claims are constituted by processes of opinion and will formation, "[h]uman rights norms assume 'flesh and blood' through democratic iterations". To Benhabib (2010, 4)

> [Even] human rights norms require interpretation, saturation and vernacularization; they cannot just be imposed by legal elites and judges upon recalcitrant peoples; rather, they must become elements in the public culture of democratic peoples through their own processes of interpretation, articulation and iteration.

For democratic iterations to be grounded in will formation, participants act with their conscience as they endeavour to provoke, confront and remonstrate with their intelligences and freedoms. Intense deliberations do not just involve public self-reflection and public defensiveness of this or that matter. It also creates opportunities for participants to act with their emotions as they engage with one another and talk back to one another. And, when humans exercise democratic reflexivity, they do not do so without an equal appeal to their intellect and emotions. Through the public expression of opinion and action, asserts Benhabib (2010, 6), the human is viewed as a creature who is capable of self-interpreting rights claims "[h]aving a right means having the capacity to initiate action and opinion to be shared by others through an interpretation of the very right claim itself". The point is that their mutual respect for views initiates processes of democratic iteration that are both linguistically and culturally informed on account of repetitive judgements in action.

As averred by Benhabib (2006, 49), democratic iterations are guided by 'will-formation' of people when they engage, contest and talk back about meanings on which they have reflected and which they have defended. The point is the pursuit of making iterations manifest in human practices; people never do so without their intelligences and emotions. To Benhabib (2010, 5), only if the people are viewed not merely as subject to the law, but also as authors of the law "can the contextualisation and interpretation of human rights be said to result from public and free processes of democratic opinion and will-formation". In other words, when humans seek to resolve their societal affairs through democratic iterations, they seek to engage with one another with hospitality and a self-determination to act justly. And, for the latter to happen, humans invariably act with intelligence, emotions and responsible human acts.

Democratic Iteration and Deepening Responsible Human Acts

Previously in this chapter, we mentioned that Benhabib (2011) views controversies as necessary for liberal democracies. She maintains that the rights and other principles of the liberal democratic state need to be challenged periodically in order to retain and enrich their original meaning, because

It is only when new groups claim that they belong within the circles of addressees of a right from which they have been excluded in its initial articulation that we come to understand the fundamental limitedness of every individual right claim within a specific constitutional tradition, as well as the context-transcending validity of such claims. (Benhabib 2011, 182)

To Benhabib (2011, 182), the democratic dialogue is "enhanced through the repositioning and rearticulation of rights in the public spheres of liberal democracies". Here, the democratic dialogue necessarily includes engagements of agreement and consensus, as much as it does disagreement and dissensus.

Like Benhabib (2011), Mouffe (2000) does not consider conflict and controversy as antagonistic to a democracy, and so the idea is not to eliminate conflict from the political arena, but to approach conflict so that it is compatible with democratic values—as in Benhabib's (2004) notion of democratic iterations. In Mouffe's (2000) opinion, if we want people to be free, we must always allow for the possibility that conflict may appear, and we should provide an arena where differences can be confronted. The case of the French scarf affair, as mentioned by Benhabib (2011) is, of course, not an isolated incident of a liberal democracy underestimating its own liberal values. What started as the expulsion of three hijab-wearing Muslim schools from their school in 1989, escalated into a mass exclusion of 23 Muslim girls from their schools in 1996 (Benhabib 2011). The ensuing controversy revolved around appeals for a separation between the state and religion, what is understood by French national identity, why Muslim women wear hijab in relation to their identity and—of course—the response of liberal democracies to minority groups. Thomassen (2011, 129) explains:

> The hijab controversies raise questions about the identity and limits of the political community, in turn touches upon the significance—the importance and the meaning—hijab: can you wear the hijab and be French at the same time? What laicite mean? and so on. The significance of the hijab is contested, and must ask who has and who does not have a voice in its signification. In this way, the question of meaning and identity is linked to that of the agency women who wear the hijab and their ability to define the meaning of what they wear.

Benhabib (2011, 172–173) explains that after nearly a decade of confrontations, the French National Assembly passed a law in 2004, "with a great majority, banning not only the wearing of the 'scarf'"—now interestingly referred to as *la voile* (the veil)—but also the wearing of all "ostentatious signs of religious belonging in the public sphere". To Benhabib (2011, 173), the significance of this "national drama" or "national trauma" is that it took a few teenagers to expose the fragility of the balance between respecting the individual's rights to freedom of conscience and religion, on the one hand, and maintaining a public sphere devoid of all religious symbolisms on the other. *L'affaire du foulard* (the scarf affair), according to Benhabib (2011, 173), "eventually came to stand for all dilemmas of French national identity in the age of globalization and multiculturalism".

Although different in content and form, the unfolding debates surrounding the scarf affair resonate in an entirely different context, such as South Africa. Many South African schools continue to be wrapped in controversy and conflict, as school leaders stumble in transitioning from practices of exclusion to inclusion, from assimilation to recognition and from authoritarian dictates to democratic engagements. In similar regulatory attempts, as seen in the scarf affair, learners at a South African girls' school were forbidden from speaking local African languages and were issued with demerits or fined R10 when caught "making those noises" (Nicholson 2016). At another girls-only school, learners were expected to carry a yellow merit book at all times. Transgressions, such as speaking Xhosa—even during break-times—were recorded as a demerit in the book (Isaacs 2016). The schools in question justified the prohibition of local African languages on the basis of promoting English. They maintain that, if the girls speak English during all their engagements and conversations, they will not only improve their language skills, but they will also have a better chance of academic success. In the opinion of the schools, the prohibition of African languages is not an indictment on those languages, but rather a means to academic achievement.

Against these Anglo-Saxon norms of what constitutes academic achievement, and how it ought to be achieved, are emotions of deep humiliation and alienation. The girls in question considered the denial of their black hair and language as denial of the self. One girl described how a teacher "instructed me to fix myself as if I was broken". She attested, "My hair is natural and connected to my roots. They are not braids, they are roots" (Pather 2016). The girls experienced conflict in being forced not only to look a certain way, but also to speak a particular language using a particular accent. Seemingly, the logic applied to black learners entering historically whites-only spaces is that they have nothing to offer these spaces. These spaces are pre-defined in relation to particular constructions of what is right and acceptable, of what holds power and what does not. Black learners with their black hairstyles and black languages are considered an intrusion that needs to be (re)-shaped in line with what is right and fixed (Davids 2018). Kenyan author Wa Thiong'o describes a similar example, relating how he was punished and humiliated for speaking his mother tongue of Gikuyu at an English-medium school. For the colonial power, he states, "[l]anguage was the means of the spiritual subjugation" (1981, 286).

Like the Muslim girls, who prompted the French scarf affair, learners in South African schools expressed outrage at being prohibited from speaking 'black languages' and for being coerced to straighten their hair. In response, a few teachers at these schools responded with their own outrage, accusing learners of being so preoccupied with issues of race and politics that they failed to take their academic progress seriously. The outrage soon descended into threats, with teachers telling learners, "[i]f you don't want to come to the school you can find another school" (Nicholson 2016). Commentaries on social media were equally critical of the learners' decision to embark on protest action, and the girls were accused and judged for not "being appreciative enough of their good education, and should return to their black schools" (Pather 2016).

One of the concerns highlighted by Benhabib (2011, 174) in relation to the scarf affair was that "[t]he girls' voices were not heard much in this heated debate, although there was a genuine public discourse in the French public sphere and some soul-searching on questions of democracy and differences in a multicultural society". As noted by Thomassen (2011, 134), the girls' silence on the matter is problematic for Benhabib (2011) insofar as democratic iterations should be a process of self-constitution rather than others defining your identity. Benhabib (2011, 174) confirms that, had the girls' voices been listened to, it would have become apparent that the meaning of wearing the hijab or scarf had changed from being a religious act to one of cultural defiance and increasing politicisation. As we take account of the two narratives of the French scarf affair and the South African language and hair incident, it becomes apparent that while the two cases are not the same, they are also not dissimilar. In both cases, there is an overt push for the girls to conform to a predetermined notion of what constitutes an acceptable dress code in the public sphere. According to

Modood (1998, 6), ideas of what constitutes acceptability is problematically couched in homogeneous constructions of identity, and creates the impression, that

> [Identities and cultures] are discrete, frozen in time, impervious to external influence, homogeneous and without internal dissent; that people of certain family, ethnic or geographical origins are always to be defined by them and indeed are supposed to be behaviourally determined by them.

For Benhabib (2010), it is important that through democratic iterations (complex processes of public argument and deliberation), new learnings and renewed understandings and action might emerge. Democratic iterations, she argues,

> [D]o not alter conditions of the normative validity of practical discourses that are established independently of them; rather, democratic iterations enable us to judge as legitimate or illegitimate the processes of opinion and will-formation through which rights claims are contextualized and contested, expanded and revised through actual institutional practices in the light of such criteria. (Benhabib 2010, 6)

In the case of the French Muslim girls, the hijab was no longer seen as an item signifying a religious identity, but as "a political symbol requiring careful state regulation and monitoring" (Benhabib 2011, 181). In turn, the ensuing controversy "touched upon the self-understanding of French republicanism for the left as well as the right, on the meaning of social and sexual equality, and liberalism vs republicanism vs multiculturalism in French life" (Benhabib 2011, 173).

In the South African case, the debate laid bare the predominance of Anglo-Saxon norms, which are used as measures of exclusion and humiliation. Moreover, the controversy revealed the challenges that learners, who constitute the minority at historically advantaged (white) schools, continue to experience, despite a context of a liberal democracy and extensive educational policies, intended to counter any form of discrimination, marginalisation and exclusion. In protesting the regulatory practices of the schools, the girls provoked not only their teachers and respective principals into reflecting what they had experienced as demeaning practices, but they also confronted educational officials for seemingly being unaware of 'hair policies', when these were freely available on their schools' websites.

Even human rights norms require interpretation, saturation and vernacularisation, argues Benhabib (2011, 4), "they cannot just be imposed by legal elites and judges upon recalcitrant peoples; rather, they must become elements in the public culture of democratic peoples through their own processes of interpretation, articulation and iteration." In voicing their outrage, frustration and disappointment, the girls were able to reflect on their experiences, and the abuse of power, as exercised by school authorities. Through iterating their conflict, the girls acted with intelligence and emotions, and by doing so, they sought to find an end to their exclusion and humiliation by appealing to the school to act justly and fairly.

Summary

This chapter focused extensively on Benhabib's (2004) conception of democratic iteration, as being at the core of democratic education. We reflected on both the public sphere as well as the school to illustrate cases of controversy and contestation in order to show, firstly, that democracy is never without conflict, and secondly, that democratic iteration allows for reconsiderations and renewal of engagements. Following Benhabib, we emphasised that the premise of democratic iterations is not to alter the normative validity of practical discourses, but to determine the legitimacy of particular processes of opinion and will formation. In this regard, we focused on two examples: one commonly referred to as 'the French scarf affair' and the other involving the prohibition of 'black languages and hair' in South African schools. We argued, considering that iterations are both rationally and emotionally conceived, that it would be unjustifiable to delink democratic education from rational articulations and rearticulations and emotional will formation. Together the rational and emotive dimensions of democratic education make it possible for human injustices to be dealt with more plausibly.

References

Benhabib, S. 1996. Towards a Deliberative Model of Democratic Legitimacy. In *Democracy and Difference: Contesting the Boundaries of the Political*, ed. S. Benhabib, 67–94. Princeton, NJ: Princeton University Press.
———. 2004. *The Rights of Others: Aliens, Residents and Citizens*. The John Robert Seeley Memorial Lectures. Cambridge: Cambridge University Press.
———. 2006. *Another Cosmopolitanism*. Oxford: Oxford University Press.

———. 2010. *Human Rights, Sovereignty and Democratic Iterations*. Session 6, Keynote Lectures: Human Rights—Global Culture—International Institutions, Our Common Future. Hannover.

———. 2011. *Dignity in Adversity: Human Rights in Troubled Times*. Cambridge: Polity Press.

Davids, N. 2018. Global Citizenship Education, Postcolonial Identities, and a Moral Imagination. In *Palgrave Handbook of Global Citizenship and Education*, ed. I. Davis, A. Peterson, D. Kiwan, C. Peck, E. Sant, L. Ho, and Y. Waghid, 193–208. New York & London: Palgrave Macmillan.

Derrida, J. 1988. *Signature, Event, Context*. Evanston: Northwestern University Press.

Isaacs, L. 2016. San Souci Girls Protest Racist Language Rules. *Cape Times*, September 1. www.iol.co.za/capetimes/sans-souci-girls-protest-racist-language-rules-2063682. Accessed 18 Mar 2019.

Modood, T. 1998. Anti-essentialism, Multiculturalism and the 'Recognition' of Religious Groups. *Journal of Political Philosophy* 6 (4): 378–399.

Mouffe, C. 2000. *The Democratic Paradox*. London: Verso.

Nicholson, G. 2016. Pretoria Girls High: A Protest Against Sacrificed Cultures and Identities. *Daily Maverick*, August 30. www.dailymaverick.co.za/.../2016-08-30-pretoria-girls-high-a-protest-against-sacrific.... Accessed 18 Mar 2019.

Pather, R. 2016. Pretoria Girls High School Pupil: I Was Instructed to Fix Myself as if I Was Broken, August 29. https://mg.co.za/article/2016-08-29-pretoria-girls-high-school-pupil-i-was-instructed-to-fix-myself-as-if-i-was-broken. Accessed 19 Mar 2019.

Thomassen, L. 2011. The Politics of Iterability: Benhabib, the Hijab, and Democratic Iterations. *Polity* 43 (1): 128–149.

Wa Thiong'o, N. 1981. *Decolonising the Mind: The Politics of Language in African Literature*. London: James Currey.

CHAPTER 3

Democratic Education and Gratitude

Abstract In this chapter, we give an account of gratitude in relation to education. By highlighting the vagueness of the concept of gratitude, we question whether it might be plausible to consider gratitude as a moral obligation, a social convention or a political obligation in relation to the state. By leaning on Derrida's conception of friendship, we argue that gratitude cannot be gratitude, if it is not extended spontaneously and without any obligation. Gratitude, therefore is unconditional, and as such does not imply any reciprocity. Such an idea of gratitude impacts democratic education in a way whereby people engage with one another without the condition of relation.

Keywords Gratitude • Moral obligation • Political obligation • Reciprocity • Unconditionality

INTRODUCTION

In this chapter, we look at the concept and practice of gratitude as a manifestation and as an expansive understanding of democratic education. As authors who were reared in traditional Muslim homes, we cannot write this chapter without reflecting upon our own socialisation into conceptions of gratitude as exemplified in our daily lives. To this end, we have been taught to live in a continuous expression of gratitude, as found in utterances, such as *al-hamdu lillah* (all praise be to God), *insha-Allah* (if God wills) and *bismillah* (in God's name). Thus, everything we tackle in our lives, and every human encounter within which we engage, should be embellished by the above utterances as a recognition that all thankfulness or gratitude should begin with an acknowledgement of a higher good who watches over humanity. That nothing in our lives would have been possible without the presence of a higher good is an understanding into which we have been socialised throughout our entire lives. And, one way of living out our gratitude towards a higher good is to live our gratitude in relation to humanity. In this sense, gratitude, we shall argue, is an emotive experience—an action—of being in the presence of other humans. As stated in a prophetic saying, "[t]o worship God as if you see Him"—*an ta'buda Allah ka annaka tara'*. At least three aspects emerge from the above idea of gratitude in relation to education:

- firstly, gratitude is a human practice of an emotional kind;
- secondly, gratitude is always relational, such as showing gratitude towards and for someone as if that person is present; and,
- thirdly, gratitude is an act of resisting umbrage in the sense that there is much to be grateful about, as opposed to showing bitterness towards this or that, especially in times of adversity.

Gratitude as a Virtue and Emotive Practice

Gratitude, according to Kant (1964, 119–120), is a sacred virtue, a duty of love people might have towards others in return for their beneficence or kindness. Gratitude is understood to involve properly honouring the person who has shown another an act of charity or benefit. In showing gratitude, which presupposes that one has actually benefited from the act of beneficence, Kant (1964) contends, one shows respect through the demonstration of appreciation. However, he cautions that the appreciation or debt of gratitude should not be viewed as a burden that should be fulfilled. Rather, according to Kant, gratitude is a moral kindness, which allows humanity to cultivate love of one another. Moreover, because of its sacredness, the violation of gratitude can "destroy the moral incentive to beneficence in its very principle" (Kant 1964, 121), which leads him to describe the act of ingratitude towards one's benefactor as one of the most detestable vices. Kant continues by saying that, as no ordinary duty, gratitude adds moral value to the world through its expression of appreciation and respect, and through its encouragement of acts of beneficence, which ultimately cultivates a love of humanity.

Drawing on Kant, White's (1999, 43) focus is not so much on a classification of gratitude as on its contribution and value to a democratic society, and this is "centrally important to being a citizen in a democratic society". To White (1999), a democratic citizen has certain dispositions, such as hope, courage, truth, honesty and gratitude—all of which enhance a democratic society. She differentiates between a debt account of gratitude and a recognition account of gratitude. A debt account, she explicates, implies that the recipient of a benefit should acknowledge the benefit or the benefactor in a fitting way. From a Kantian perspective, this should best be avoided, since it places the individual in a position where he or she is obliged to show gratitude (Kant 1979, 222). As an alternative to a debt account, White (1999) argues for a recognition account, which retains the elements of a benefactor and of a beneficiary, as well as the idea of appropriate feelings between them, but has a flexible attitude towards the motives of the benefactor and comprises what might count as an appropriate response from the beneficiary. She explains that the element of mutual recognition (between benefactor and beneficiary) might be common to both a debt and a recognition account, but within the latter, the beneficiary is seen as the repository of someone's goodwill rather than as debt. The recognition account, according to White (1999), encourages individuals to care and be cared for, to cultivate a beneficent circle of gratitude among individuals and communities, thereby enhancing conceptions of democratic citizenship.

To Klosko (1989, 355), however, gratitude has generally been taken to give rise to a rather vague obligation. Klosko (1991, 33) concedes that there is obviously a close connection between political obligations and the receipt of benefits from the state. However, he argues that the difficulty for political obligations based on gratitude "is that a theory of political obligation demands a specific response; the recipient is not under a *general* obligation to express his [or her] gratitude to the state in some appropriate way but has a *specific* obligation to obey the law" (Klosko 1991, 34). As noted by Klosko (1991), theorists are doubtful about the propriety of extending the concept of gratitude from the private sphere of interpersonal relations to the public, political sphere. For example, White (1999), on the one hand, believes that citizens ought not to be grateful for what is due to them as a right, and should not be expected to express gratitude to a government, which has been elected for the express purpose of serving a democratic agenda. On the other hand, Weiss (1985, 491) holds that because of the unspecific content of gratitude—which is largely defined by social convention—it is less compliant with a rigid moral obligation and more commensurable with a category of social graces.

In addition, gratitude theory faces more comprehensive objections in that the very idea of *expecting* someone to respond with gratitude is problematic. It is essential to gratitude, asserts Klosko (1991, 44), "that the grateful response by gratuitous: spontaneous and *not* required". Hence, it might be argued that gratitude is a desired response when an individual shows kindness, but in order for gratitude to be one of genuine gratefulness, it has to be voluntary and spontaneous. Klosko (1991, 44) continues that an action performed from gratitude is necessarily performed in a certain way:

> It is not merely an action but an action performed because of certain feelings, especially the desire to make one's appreciation known to the benefactor (the demonstrative requirement) and to behave in a certain way towards him, because one has regard for him and does not view him merely as a means to one's own satisfaction (the substantive requirement).

It is the emotive element, implicit within gratitude, which problematises a gratitude theory of political obligation. As Klosko (1991, 45) explains, the state does not require that we have certain feelings but that we behave in certain ways, which renders the idea of an expression of gratitude questionable.

Now that we have highlighted the vagueness of gratitude in relation to some of the dominant debates, we continue by providing a deconstructive analysis of the term 'gratitude' in relation to education and how it potentially affects higher education. Our contention is that if we look at gratitude differently, it might just be that our democratic relations with students might be deepened and, by implication, more trust might ensue.

Gratitude as an Unconditional Act of Giving Without Receiving

Both of us have been involved with doctoral supervision throughout the course of our professional careers. Generally, we embark on these supervision journeys with enthusiasm and commitment to ensure a successful completion of the study, and hence, qualification. Not only are students supported with regular one-to-one engagements, but they also receive regular and substantive feedback on their progress, are invited to various postgraduate programmes and, if funding permits, are encouraged to attend both local and international conferences. The point is that we consider supervision not only as necessary for a student's academic progress, but also as an enhancement of our own scholarship. After five years (in most cases), when the journey comes to an end, we reflect on the thesis and its significance as much as we reflect on the type of relationship that had evolved on account of the student–supervisor relationship. Of course, none of these relationships are ever the same. Like teaching and learning, the supervision process is entirely relational, but generally, we enjoy what we would describe as respectful, enjoyable and productive relationships.

Invariably, however, when we engage in our students' progress and attitudes, we come to the same conclusion: irrespective of how diligent we have been throughout our supervision of students' studies, we seem to be disappointed and troubled by what we perceive to be their apparent lack of gratitude for their supervision. In a number on instances, students are simply never heard from again once they completed their viva voce. In many ways, we seem to be emotionally touched by what we interpret as a lack of gratitude displayed on the part of many students towards our rigorous and caring supervision of their work. Such a position of discomfort seems to be spurred on by a lack of indebtedness shown by students towards us, although we feel that we have supervised them with dignity, respect, empathy and justice.

As we write this chapter, we duly ask ourselves why we have these expectations. Students might, quite correctly, respond that they pay exorbitant fees, and that showing gratitude is not incumbent on them. They might equally assert that supervision is our job, for which we get paid—so why is gratitude necessary? Our own response is that we nevertheless expect students to show gratitude, because most of our research is immersed in democratic citizenship education, which means that everything we deliberate upon pivots on central themes of principled actions, which include gratitude. On the one hand, we therefore interpret the neglect of students to express gratitude as a deficiency in their capacity or willingness to internalise conceptions of democratic citizenship education. On the other hand, we question what we could and should have done differently to ensure that students find meaning and expression through their research, so that the study and resultant thesis adopts a humane significance instead of only textual evidence of writing. We have these conversations and reflections with the students in a university context, which is often not only alienating, but also highly competitive as students compete for access and navigate considerable odds in affording and sustaining their studies. It is in this regard that we agree with Kerry Howells (2012, 6) when she avers that academic environments are breeding grounds for conditions that make it difficult for gratitude and trust to flourish. In her words

> Conditions that are the antithesis to gratitude—resentment, victim mentality, envy or a sense of entitlement are toxins that kill off goodwill. A toxic environment of ensuing complaint culminates in good teachers and students walking out wounded by ingratitude, extremely unlikely to return. It is our lack of consciousness of the impact of this malaise that keeps us in the dark, and stops many wonderful education initiatives from taking hold. (Howells 2012, 6)

Consider the example of a student who decided to convert his or her successfully completed doctoral thesis into a book on the advice and support of the supervisor. While the student acknowledged the influence of another academic and offered gratitude in this respect, the supervisor was not mentioned. This might have been an oversight on the part of the student or the student might have been negligent in acknowledging the supervisor. However, to have mentioned an academic other than the supervisor in the text could be interpreted as an instance of ingratitude shown towards the supervisor. Such a situation brings to the fore two questions: should supervisors be concerned when they are not shown gratitude by students? And, should supervisors have the expectation that they should be shown gratitude? About the first question, a sensitive supervisor might interpret the student's act of omitting to acknowledge him or her as deeply troubling in the sense that not recognising the supervisor's influence on the student's work could give the impression that the supervisor had no influence over the published study. Not acknowledging the supervisor's role could be misinterpreted as a student's intention to delink his study from the supervisor and perhaps as an opportunity for the student to show his or her dissatisfaction with the supervision. In this instance, the supervisor should be concerned that his or her efforts at supervision have been gravely misconstrued.

Other examples have nothing to do with student supervision. Often, we are faced with students who are experiencing financial or emotional troubles, which prevent them from attending to their studies adequately. In one instance, a student, who had a dismal attendance record because of all sorts of reasons, and barely submitted her required assignments, eventually failed three of her modules. This caused her much distress, specifically because she did not have the funds to sustain her studies for another year. As a compassionate and caring response, one of us went to great lengths to get other academics to support her by allowing her to submit late assignments and providing one-on-one tutoring so that she could complete the minimum requirements for her degree. Despite her being aware of the concessions made for her, she did not show any gratitude and was never heard from again once she realised that she had passed the three modules.

The point being made here is not to bemoan the ingratitude of students. That in itself would reveal our own ingratitude. Rather, we want to consider what we might do differently. For this reason, we thought it apposite to look at Jacques Derrida's neo-Aristotelian analysis of friendship and then to connect it to the practice of gratitude.

Gratitude as an Act of Friendship

In the first place, the expression, *al-hamdu lillah* (all praise be to God) seems to intimate that gratefulness should be shown only towards a higher good. However, if one considers that this same higher good is responsible for human creation, then one way of showing gratitude towards God, is to acknowledge those whom He had created. Thus, showing gratitude to humans implicitly accentuates gratitude being shown to God. Therefore, the notion that humans should not be the recipients of thankfulness seems to be a misplaced and indefensible idea. The question is not a matter of whether humans should be shown gratitude. Rather, can gratitude be shown differently, that is, other than directly acknowledging the one who should receive gratitude? For such a discussion, we now turn to Derrida's (1997) idea of friendship.

Drawing on Aristotle's idea of friendship, Derrida (1997, 8) offers a notion of friendship whereby "it is advisable to love rather than to be loved". So, for Derrida (1997, 8), the act of friendship consists in loving, or "to love *before* being loved". In his words, "one must know that the only way to find out is by questioning first of all the act and the experience of loving rather than the state or situation of being loved" (Derrida 1997, 8). Thus, for Derrida, a friend is a "person who loves before being the person who is loved: he [or she] who loves before being the beloved" (Derrida 1997, 9). Like a friend who offers love without the expectation of being loved in return, we surmise that someone who shows genuine gratitude does not have to expect gratitude in return. As a friend who loves without being loved in return, a person who shows gratitude is genuinely thankful without the condition that gratitude be reciprocated. Derrida's (1997) argument in defence of the one who loves or shows gratitude has some connection with the limit of possibility—that is, in order to love, a person has to be alive, and such love can be for a deceased being as well. By implication, when a dead person is loved, there cannot be the expectation on the part of the one who loves to actually be loved in return. Hence, loving (friendship) begins "with the possibility of survival" (Derrida 1997, 13) for the one who loves or the friend should be alive to show love or gratitude and, when the person being shown gratitude towards is not alive, there cannot be any expectation that the person being loved should reciprocate love or should love in return.

Similar to the notion of friendship or loving, a person who shows gratitude does so when he or she expresses his or her thankfulness towards someone else. But the expectation should never be that one's act of showing gratitude is conditional upon someone else returning gratitude. Like a genuine friend who loves another person should not expect to be loved in return, so the act of gratitude is not dependent on another person returning gratitude. The act of gratitude lies in the intention and act of the person showing gratitude. What follows from the aforementioned understanding of gratitude is that the act of showing gratitude is unconditional in the sense that showing gratitude does not depend on gratitude being returned to the one who shows it. An example of showing gratitude is when a student expresses his or her thankfulness towards his or her deceased supervisor who cannot return gratitude. Moreover, genuine gratitude happens when a person thanks another without the expectation that gratitude would be returned—that is a gratitude "without presence [of another's thankfulness]" (Derrida 1997, 155).

If we contextualise the above understanding of gratitude in relation to our own supervision, then we should not be perturbed when students do not return gratitude for the reason that legitimate gratitude does not depend on what others do, but more on the act of gratitude we show. As aptly stated by Derrida (1997, 195), genuine friendship—and we would argue gratitude—is shown when "I entrust myself without measure, to the other. I entrust myself to him [or her] more than to myself, he [or she] is in me before me and more than me". In a way, gratitude, following Derrida (1997, 203), is a risk one takes, in other words, "a sort of trust without contract", a form of gratitude based on virtue. Gratitude, like friendship, is a virtue because it is constituted by intention, will and choice of a person who shows his or her thankfulness without asking to be thanked in return. We are reminded by Derrida (1997, 223), "[ethical] friendship [like gratitude] orders me to love the other [to be thankful to the other] as he [or she] is while wishing that he [or she] remain as he [or she] is [that is, without expecting him or her to return his or her love or gratitude]". Thus, gratitude is about a virtuous thought of the other for what he or she has done for one, without the expectation that the other would or should return gratitude. In supervising students, we should be concerned only with guiding, mentoring and supporting students throughout the completion of their studies. And, the expectation should not be there that they (students) have to be thankful to us for supervising them. In the event that students do things that could be interpreted as a violation of the trust we had in them, we should not even be disappointed, if we have shown genuine gratitude. Gratitude is what we offer and show as supervisors without the expectation that students would reciprocate gratitude. Put differently, under the conditions of gratitude, a person who shows gratitude is a giver and not a receiver of gratitude. This brings us to a discussion of how gratitude could enhance democratic education.

Gratitude and an Enactment of Democratic Education

Showing gratitude is about recognising the other, such as when one shows respect for the other in his or her presence. Such a relationship whereby one shows gratitude is not always a reciprocal one in the sense that one does not have to receive gratitude in return. In a Derridean way, it is a relationship without a relation (Derrida 1997, 298). A relationship grounded in an ethics of gratitude is therefore a relationship where one shows one's capability to respect the other person freely without expecting to be shown respect in return. A student who does not show gratitude in return to his or her supervisor, but remains in a relationship with his or her supervisor who shows him or her much gratitude, does not reciprocate gratitude and is in no relation with his or her supervisor. Hence, showing gratitude implies a risk one takes to be in a relationship without relation.

Such a notion of gratitude turns the practice of democratic education upside down: democratic education can no longer be such that one's relationship with another person is reciprocal, but rather one where risk is always present. A relationship of gratitude implies that the one who expresses gratitude is without a relation in the sense that he or she does not expect to be shown gratitude in return. It is not a relationship of reciprocity. Instead, it is a risky one because the possibility is always there that the one being shown gratitude does not equally return gratitude. Yet, the risk in the relationship is that there is no relation—it might still come but it is not yet there. What is more, if one thinks of democratic education along the lines of being at risk, one invariably recognises the possibility that such a relationship (democratic education) "remains to come" (Derrida 1997, 306). In other words, the risk of democratic education is that it "remain[s] indefinitely imperfectible, hence always insufficient and future, but belonging to the time of the promise, it will always remain … to come" (Derrida 1997, 306).

Like gratitude, which is there but does not exist, as it is never reciprocally present, democratic education remains open to the "come", which always occasions in people a surge of gratitude (Derrida 1997, 302). The advantage of such an understanding of democratic education is that it remains open to the risk that participants will engage in a relationship without relation—that is, a community without community (Derrida 1997, 298). In this sense, democratic education cannot be about a desire to engage people in "the order of the common or the community, the share taken up or given, participation or sharing" (Derrida 1997, 298). Instead, democratic education should be concerned with not keeping people in common, but rather in ruptures through which they are always capable of becoming enriched, open to the impossible and ready for an experience of freedom and equality (Derrida 1997, 306).

Summary

In this chapter, we have given an account of gratitude in relation to education. By highlighting the vagueness of the concept of gratitude, we questioned whether it might be considered a moral obligation, a social convention or a political obligation, when considered in relation to the state. Taking different viewpoints into account, we argued that gratitude is an act of emotion—that is, "an action performed because of certain feelings" (Klosko 1991, 44). By leaning on Derrida's conception of friendship, we argued that gratitude cannot be gratitude if it is not extended spontaneously and without any obligation. Gratitude, therefore is unconditional, and as such, does not imply any reciprocity. Such an idea of gratitude affects democratic education in a way whereby people engage with one another without the condition of relations. In other words, democratic education is about taking a risk that people remain in a relationship without a relation—that is, they engage in a community without community. In the next chapter, we look at how other emotions, such as belligerence and distress, influence democratic education.

References

Derrida, J. 1997. *Politics of Friendship*. Trans. G. Collins. London: Verso.
Howells, K. 2012. *Gratitude in Education: A Radical View*. Rotterdam: Sense.
Kant, I. 1964. *The Metaphysical Principles of Virtue*. New York: Bobbs-Merrill.
———. 1979. *Lectures on Ethics*. London: Methuen.
Klosko, G. 1989. Political Obligation and Gratitude. *Philosophy & Public Affairs* 18 (4): 352–358.
———. 1991. Four Arguments Against Political Obligations from Gratitude. *Public Affairs Quarterly* 5 (1): 33–48.
Weiss, R. 1985. The Moral and Social Dimensions of Gratitude. *Southern Journal of Philosophy* 23 (4): 491–501.
White, P. 1999. Gratitude, Citizenship and Education. *Studies in Philosophy and Education* 18 (1/2): 43–52.

CHAPTER 4

Belligerence and Distress as Emotions in Democratic Education

Abstract In this chapter, we show how democratic education encourages respect, mutual engagement and the recognition of a plurality of views. Inasmuch as reasonable persons engage deliberatively with one another, they invariably draw on their emotions as they endeavour to reason together. Yet, when reasonable people engage openly and freely they take responsibility for one another's views. Even when they are provoked by the emotions of distress and belligerence, they are responsible enough to make sure to restrain their hostility towards one another that potentially leads to open conflict. Rather, their belligerence and distress allow them to speak their minds without being silenced even when their views are provocative and dissenting. Through speech participants disturb doubts about the claims being proffered and collectively strive together to achieve conciliation when rival positions are taken into perspective.

Keywords Respect • Mutual engagement • Recognition • Plurality • Reasonableness • Dissent

INTRODUCTION

One of us taught a critical pedagogy class for postgraduate students. Confronted by criticisms from colleagues who felt that critique and provocation have no place in teaching and learning, it somehow happened that teaching collapsed into some mechanical exercise during which students were told what do and where they had to consider using their own voices as unwarranted in learning. We, however, regard the suppression of student voices as uneducational not only in pedagogical encounters but also in terms of the advancement of democratic citizenship education. Hence, our focus will now shift to a justification for why belligerence ought to find its way into a tenable form of democratic education. In the previous chapters, we argued that emotive action constitutes democratic education. Inasmuch as democratic education is underscored by rational human action, it is equally guided by human emotions. In this chapter, we examine why and how belligerence and distress manifest in democratic educational practices, in the same way freedom, iteration and gratitude unfold in such actions. For an elucidation of belligerence and distress in human action, we turn to the seminal ideas of Eamonn Callan (1997).

Moral Distress as a Dialogical Endeavour

In the first place, considering that different people engage with one another on the basis of their different cultures—people's forms of life— these people invariably enact their capacities towards the adoption of new perspectives, new ways of questioning and a revision of existing practices (Waldron 2003). Following Waldron (2003, 234), people belonging to a particular culture generally endorse what they have learned within their cultures, and it is practically impossible to isolate an individual from the culture in which he or she has been cultivated. In this sense, when people are socialised or acculturated into particular norms and traditions, it would be difficult for them to question or contest such norms. For example, an individual reared in a home governed by and immersed in patriarchal understandings of the world would not easily be able to act contrary to these understandings.

Often, what people learn within their cultures is extended to and accepted in their adult lives. A number of students in our philosophy of education class, for instance, have been reared in cultures where the use of corporal punishment is an acceptable form of discipline. Their continuing support of corporal punishment is advocated through an understanding that it worked for them and that they turned out fine, which means corporal punishment is not a bad action. Attempts to get these students to consider alternatives are at times met with serious resistance, as they interpret it as an attempt to undermine their cultures. It is difficult, therefore, to constrain an individual in relation to exercising his or her cultural liberty. To this end, those who are confronted belligerently in encounters would find it challenging to contend with human confrontation and contestation. The fact that our students, for example, feel affronted about our questioning of corporal punishment, causes them some distress, because they interpret our questioning as provocatively bringing their cultures into disrepute. Hence, their response to what they perceive as our belligerence prevents them from speaking freely, because they also have to deal with their own emotional agitation. As Waldron (2003, 29) intimates, cultural encounters are rarely smooth and just. Human encounters are provocative, contestable and distressful. Here, Eamonn Callan (1997, 201–202) reminds us that, "real moral dialogue [through human encounters], as opposed to carefully policed conversations … cannot occur without the risk of offence, an offence-free school [or university] would oblige us to eschew dialogue". We shall now look at how necessary moral distress is in an enactment of democratic education.

Firstly, Callan (1997, 204) avers that in a democracy, those who engage in matters pertaining to education—whether racism, censorship or human injustice—should recognise the "gravity of what is at stake". We concur with Callan's (1997, 204) justification that "the gravity of what is at stake" should prevail over the narcissistic importance of humans for the latter would be concerned with how much prestige we win or lose in an encounter. Yet, what can ensue from "the heat of [distressful] dialectical conflict … [is] moral truth" (Callan 1997, 204). In his words

> In fact, the very idea that we might treat the other and our relationship to the other as 'more important' than the topic of moral dialogue cannot be right given [the] … argument that strong critical commitment to virtue is constitutive of the virtuous self. Consider how serious moral deliberation and dialogue look when we examine them from the perspective of a moral conception that takes the claims of virtue seriously. (Callan 1997, 204)

The more truth is probed the more humans in encounters become restive as they endeavour to uncover "the gravity of what is at stake" (Callan 1997, 204). And, as humans endeavour to make bare what is concealed, they become agitated and uneasy, often resulting in angst for the participants. Encounters hence become increasingly confrontational—that is, belligerent. As aptly put by Mill (1869, cited in Callan 1997, 210), "in the great practical concerns of life … [truth] has to be made by the rough process of struggle between combatants fighting under hostile banners". At the time of writing, an academic in our faculty has been embroiled in conflict with one of her classes, in which she has been confronted for teaching in Afrikaans—a language, which a number of students cannot understand. They have dismissed the use of translation serves as provided for within the language policy of the university. Discussions with the academic and specifically attempts to get her to reconsider her medium of instruction for the sake of ensuring the inclusion of all students have only lead to a deepening of the confrontation. At stake for her is not only an issue of language but her identity. That she is being asked not to teach in Afrikaans has been experienced as a denial of her identity as an Afrikaner, and hence, her intense distress and alienation.

Secondly, when distress is provoked in participants by confrontation, such as when a colleague attempts to undermine another by coming up with unnecessary and rival ways to improve academic performance, this "may also be a sign of disturbing (and not necessarily conscious) doubts about the correctness of our moral beliefs or about the importance of the differences what we and others believe" (Callan 1997, 211). It could well be that the moral distress encountered may result in "emotional turmoil … [that could end up in] humiliated silence or a fearful withdrawal from the dialogical fray" (Callan 1997, 212). However, because moral uncertainty has been inserted in a human encounter, it can be concluded that progress has already been made in the sense that doubts about what we believe are true and have been appended in the encounter. Although one might therefore consider the interruption of additional thoughts in the encounter about improving academic performance—especially if such ideas come from a usually combative person—as distressful and injudicious at first, one could perhaps begin to see the judicial worthiness of such a view as the encounter unfolds and more confrontational views are infused in the encounter. Invariably then, such a distressful encounter could be advantageous for the process of evaluating academic performance.

Thirdly, as cogently argued for by Callan (1997, 222), moral friction and distress coerce participants in conversations to deliberate more publicly to the extent that they have to distinguish reasonable conceptions from unreasonable ones of value. In other words, belligerent confrontation has the educational benefit that pluralistic views will be respected collectively to avoid ethical regression that pulls us away from dialogue (Callan 1997, 220). Ethical confrontation creates possibilities for participants to become more open-minded, as there are many controversies and a plurality of opinions to consider (Callan 1997, 216). And, as dialogue proceeds, "the distress and belligerence of confrontation will naturally give way to conciliation as moral truth is pieced together from the fragmentary insights of conflicting viewpoints" (Callan 1997, 214–215). As stated by Callan (1997, 215) once more:

> By a different kind of conciliation I mean this: the fitting response to ongoing moral conflict is sometimes not renewed effort to achieve dialogical victory over our adversaries but rather the attempt to find and enact terms of political coexistence that we and they can reasonably endorse as morally acceptable.

In sum, the point about belligerence and distress in democratic educational encounters is that combat and intellectual intimidation eventually give way to ethical conciliation when argumentative judgements in rival positions become increasingly transparent and a tenable synthesis of opposing views has been achieved (Callan 1997, 212).

In Defence of Belligerence and Distress in Education

The territory of a university, as any academic will confirm, is never without distress and belligerence. The nature of the academic world is such that experiences of competitiveness, rivalry, suspicion and undermining are always simmering in one or another—not only among academics but between academics and students, and among students. We are reminded of a recent example where a postgraduate student brought into question the examination process of her master's thesis. As per university protocol, her thesis was subjected to two examiners, followed by a viva voce. While one of the examiners awarded her a very favourable report and result, the other did not, and substantiated this assessment with a detailed report. On the one hand, the student expressed her dismay and disappointment at the second examiner's poor assessment of her thesis. On the other hand, she was keen for the viva voce to take place, as she expected it to allow her the space and opportunity to defend her thesis, and hopefully, get the second examiner to reconsider his initial report.

The viva voce, however, did not unfold in the manner as expected by the student. The second examiner exhibited a reluctance to engage with her on his report, as he felt that he had already clarified his assessment. He was only interested in understanding how the student planned to address his questions and concerns. Because the student was intent on defending her thesis, she was not adequately prepared to provide the examiner with a clear indication of how the revisions would be approached. The student's expectation that the viva voce would somehow provide her with an opportunity to redeem her thesis, and hence her hard work, quickly descended into a distressful educational encounter. As she wrote in her subsequent grievance, she felt unheard and dismissed, and wished to request another opportunity to state her case. After lodging her initial grievance with her supervisor, she escalated her complaint to the chairperson of the department. The response from the departmental chairperson was that the examination process had been fair, procedures had been followed and that the second examiner had provided ample substantiation and justification for his report. That the student had the expectation that the examiner would be more engaging and open to listening to her could not be used as a reason or justification for her allegations of an unfair process. The student, however, persisted in her belligerence, and took her grievance to the vice-dean, then to the dean, and finally, to the rector.

In each of her ensuing grievance letters, the strain of her emotional distress became more and more evident. What started as an initial dissatisfaction with the viva voce, changed into allegations of unfair treatment and, eventually, discrimination. The student, however, was not the only one feeling distressed. One of us, who was directly involved in this incident, began to doubt whether the student had indeed been treated fairly. Was the student adequately prepared for the viva voce? Should more have been done to prepare her not for only what might have happened, but also for what might not happen? Should the examiner have been asked to listen to what the student had to say—specifically, to allow the student to present a counter-argument to his report? Should the student have been listened to more, not just by the examiner, but also by her supervisor and the departmental chair? Was enough cognisance given to how difficult it must have been for the student to counter her examination reports, in the first place? Did the entire educational process created provide sufficient opportunity for her to voice her dissent and to deliberate with those she was questioning? The fact that the student was visibly distressed and had experienced the viva voce as discriminatory, created a deep sense of having let the student down, that, in fact, she had been wronged. In this regard, we are reminded of Levinson's (2015, 207) contention that academics and teachers suffer moral injury, when despite a wholehearted desire to act justly, the allegation of perpetrating a moral wrong persists. To Levinson (2015, 210), "moral injury will never be fully eliminated, nor should it be, as it is generated by an appropriately progressive moral engagement. When one egregious form of systemic injustice is eliminated, previously overlooked injustices may become visible." Levinson (2015, 227) argues:

> Moral injury is brought about by being in a position invested with moral responsibility and authority but being unable to satisfy those responsibilities—and in fact, finding oneself perpetrating acts that significantly wrong others. The trauma of perpetrating significant moral wrong against others is a moral injury suffered by the perpetrator herself, distinct from the wrong done to the original victims.

When teachers and students engage deliberatively with an orientation to show dissent, the encounter invariably requires more persuasive reasons for participants to be convinced by one another's perspectives (Callan 1997). The fact that the student described her experience as discriminatory, raised an ethical dilemma, and hence, an ethical confrontation (Callan 1997, 209). Ethical confrontation as a consequence of tolerating dissent, states Callan (1997, 210), "sustains our personal investment in the truths that really matter and reminds us of their full significance by showing us vividly what it means to speak and live against them". Ethical confrontation in educational encounters, he continues, arouses distress whereby teachers and students disturb doubts about the correctness of their moral beliefs (Callan 1997, 211).

To Callan (1997, 215), the point about tolerating belligerent action "is about learning to think wisely about the difference between reasonable and unreasonable pluralism, and so far as unreasonable pluralism is part of our lives, there is much that we cannot agree to disagree about". It is a challenge for educational encounters that participants (teachers and students) exercise intellectual insight and discernment towards unreasonable utterances that threaten open-mindedness, free expression and respect for plurality of opinions (Callan 1997, 216). When academics or supervisors lay claim to a kind of moral authority over students, when they (students) question how a thesis is examined, or why they are not allowed to voice their arguments in a viva voce, academics run the risk of acting with impunity and stifling dissent, thereby constraining the educational encounter. Disagreement and ethical confrontation are constitutive of educational encounters and are necessary, argues Callan (1997, 218), to ensure "a more circumscribed and disciplined kind of deliberation that will respect the limit of reasonable disagreement when questions of political coercion are at stake".

In the end, while the student's allegations of unfair treatment or discrimination were found to be without any basis, her belligerence did not cease. Instead, she questioned what her postgraduate studies were about, what she was supposed to have learnt and whether she would consider pursuing any further studies. The exhaustion of the grievance process did not signal the end for the student, as she persisted in seeking answers for herself. As Callan (1997, 22) observes, when teachers and students engage deliberatively with an orientation to show dissent, the encounter invariably requires more persuasive reasons for participants to be convinced by one another's perspectives. In an ethical confrontation, Callan (1997, 209) argues that, no one has the right to silence dissent. Ethical confrontation as a consequence of tolerating dissent, he continues, "sustains our personal investment in the truths that really matter and reminds us of their full significance by showing us vividly what it means to speak and live against them" (Callan 1997). The point we are making is that a tolerance of dissent enhances belligerence in educational encounters that eventually paves the way for conciliation on the basis that "moral truth is pieced together from the fragmentary insights of conflicting viewpoints" (Callan 1997, 215).

It was not clear at the time of writing whether the student had reached a point of conciliation, although this is not the point of deliberation. What matters is that the student was afforded the right to confront academics ethically and she was allowed to speak her truth. To Gutmann and Ben-Porath (2015, 1), "[t]he fact of pluralism may generate a robust public debate of multiple perspectives from which all can learn, making the democratic whole even greater than the sum of its individual parts". However, they caution that, "pluralism can also create a cacophonous fragmentation that divides a democracy" (Gutmann and Ben-Porath 2015, 1). It is therefore important that, when the distress becomes evident and when the conflict unfolds, those involved exercise mutual respect and trust. People, states Levinson (2015, 21):

> [M]ake decisions in contexts rather than vacuums, embedded in webs of relationships, sensitive (perhaps overly so) to particularities and nuances, adopting roles and perspectives that are situational rather than universal. This doesn't mean operating in a merely subjectivist nor a radically particularist

frame. Values such as equality, fairness, liberty, integrity, mutual respect, and human welfare must come into play. So must considerations of rights, duties, and consequences. But nonetheless, the reasoning about them flows as much from contextual knowledge and pluralistic reflections on the problem as from references to ideal theories.

The point of engaging in an ethical confrontation is not necessarily to arrive at a mutually beneficial decision or outcome (although that would be ideal), but rather to give recognition to the right to contestation and dissent and then the right to persuasion and deliberation.

Summary

In this chapter, we have shown how democratic education encourages respect, mutual engagement and the recognition of a plurality of views. Inasmuch as reasonable persons engage deliberatively with one another, they invariably draw on their emotions as they endeavour to reason together. Yet, when reasonable people engage openly and freely they take responsibility for one another's views. Even when they are provoked by the emotions of distress and belligerence, they are responsible enough to make sure to restrain their hostility towards one another, which potentially could lead to open conflict. Rather, their belligerence and distress allow them to speak their minds without being silenced, even when their views are provocative and dissenting. Through speech, participants disturb doubts about the claims being proffered and collectively they strive together to achieve conciliation when rival positions are taken into perspective.

References

Callan, E. 1997. *Creating Citizens: Political Education and Liberal Democracy.* Oxford: Clarendon Press.
Gutmann, A., and S. Ben-Porath. 2015. Democratic Education. In *The Encyclopedia of Political Thought*, ed. M.T. Gibbons, 1–12. London: Wiley.
Levinson, M. 2015. Moral Injury and the Ethics of Educational Injustice. *Harvard Educational Review* 85 (2): 203–228.
Waldron, J. 2003. Teaching Cosmopolitan Right. In *Education and Citizenship in Liberal-Democratic Societies*, ed. K. McDonough and W. Feinberg, 23–55. New York: Oxford University Press.

CHAPTER 5

Democratic Education and Compassion

Abstract In this chapter, we analyse compassion as an emotive action in relation to democratic education—by paying specific attention to the student–supervisor relationship in relation to doctoral studies. We commence by providing insights into the types of challenges doctoral students typically present during their studies—highlighting the reality that for many of them, the external constraints brought about through socio-economic constraints and political strife both at home in their host countries often outweigh the internal demands of doctoral studies. For this reason, we argue that doctoral supervision cannot be limited to a reliance on constructions of rational argumentation and analyses, but necessarily involves emotive interactions seeped in capacities for compassionate action. Drawing on the seminal ideas of Martha Nussbaum, we show, firstly, that compassion can be construed as an emotive judgement; secondly, acting compassionately is tantamount to recognising the vulnerabilities of others and to do something about changing unsatisfactory human conditions; and thirdly, compassionate action is about enhancing democratic relations among people that can cultivate human flourishing.

Keywords Compassion • Democratic iteration • Human flourishing • Human vulnerability

Introduction

In this chapter, we discuss compassion as an emotive action in relation to democratic education. We are often confronted with candidates who are inadequately prepared for doctoral studies: poor articulation capacity, weak writing skills, lack of adherence to technical conventions of writing and funding challenges—some ostensible constraints in the pursuit of doctoral education. Yet, students remain determined to pursue their studies. As a result, we—as supervisors—are often expected to support our students in various ways—at times, in ways that might be out of the ordinary. The university where we are based is intent on establishing itself as a globally responsive research-intensive institution. As such, it not only enjoys extensive collaborations and partnerships with a range of international universities but also expends a lot of energy in locating itself as the preferred research university on the African continent. In attracting students from diverse geographical, cultural and social settings, academics are exposed to a myriad of complexities, which become an inevitable part of the doctoral journey.

In this chapter, we consider firstly some of the reasons we proffer in supporting students and, secondly, how the notion of compassion seems to extend the practice of democratic education. Thirdly, we argue why compassionate democratic education, particularly on the African continent, seems to be a tenable way to enhance democratic justice.

In Support of Student Supervision

To act compassionately towards someone implies that one has to do something for someone who might be experiencing a vulnerability of some kind. This means that one recognises that someone else might be in a vulnerable position. In turn, the vulnerability of others causes one to respond to their unfavourable situation—a matter of wanting to address such persons' vulnerabilities. The fact that one is prompted by reasons to respond to others' seemingly vulnerable situations evokes in one emotive feelings of concern for the other and his or her progress (say in doctoral studies) other than feeling pity for such persons. And, following Martha Nussbaum (2001, 19), responding to others' situations say of vulnerability involves making emotive judgements. Judgement implies that one either accepts or rejects the way things appear to one. That is, "appearance … is judgment, and that act of acceptance [or rejection] is what judgment is" (Nussbaum 2001, 37). This brings us to a discussion of compassion in relation to emotive judgement: according to Nussbaum (2001, 321), compassion comprises three cognitive elements:

> [T]he judgment of *size* (a serious bad event has befallen someone); the judgment of *nondesert* (this person did not bring the suffering on himself or herself); and the *eudaimonistic judgment* (this person, or creature, is a significant element in my scheme of goals and projects, and end whose good is to be promoted).

In the example involving some of our doctoral students, our eudaimonistic judgement of compassion is based on a number of interrelated reasons. Firstly, we recognise that doctoral students achieving their qualifications are significant for the financial sustainability of the faculty and our reasons for promoting them is linked instrumentally to their success. This is very much the situation in all South African universities that rely on state subsidy for their financial viability. And, it makes sense to exercise some eudaimonistic judgement on compassionate grounds in relation to providing student support in the pursuit of doctoral qualifications. Secondly, the majority of the doctoral students in our faculty are, in fact, not from South Africa, but from elsewhere on the African continent. These students, who come from a host of predominantly Southern African countries, are often funded by either their respective governments, or donor agencies, and are intent on studying at research universities. The attraction of research universities is that they

- possess the necessary infrastructure, such as libraries, laboratories and information technology;
- employ high-quality academic staff, generally holding PhDs;
- ensure the appropriate working conditions;
- select the best students available; and
- combine their research function with training future generations of scholars and researchers (Altbach 2013).

Despite the type of environment conducive to studying and doing research, as described here, the students often arrive with huge gaps in their understanding of educational research, Moreover, and this is the greater concern, they are often unprepared for the academic rigour which a doctoral programme demands. For supervisors, this not only means copious amounts of time spent on revising drafts upon drafts of writing, but also an emotional labour, which involves mentoring and supporting students who are away from their homes for up to five years, without an option of visiting, due to financial constraints.

Thirdly, we consider postgraduate supervision as an extension of our scholarship, where we mentor and nurture students in relation to educational theory, research methodologies and argumentation. By enacting our academic responsibilities towards our students, we are also confirming our commitment to the arena of scholarship of which we are a part. In this sense, we consider student supervision as a dialogical process through which new ways of thinking and new academics are brought to fruition. As such, supervision is not only critical to knowledge production, but also to *how* students understand academic mentoring and research. According to Henderson (2018, 403), research confirms that supervisors draw their ideas on doctoral pedagogy from a number of sources, including 'how-to' literature, their own experiences of being supervised, observing colleagues and being an examiner.

As Henderson (2018, 404) explains, research on doctoral supervision or doctoral pedagogy reveals that "supervising doctoral research is a psychosocial process that plays out in rational and irrational ways" and "it is impossible to eradicate the psychosocial irrationality of doctoral research" (see also Grant 2008). It is perhaps a sign of the times, Henderson continues, that much of the more recent doctoral supervision research seeks to increase the knowledge about supervision in order to reduce the potential for trauma. Henderson (2018, 404) asserts that the underlying assumption of many 'how-to' guides on doctoral supervision is that, if supervisors are more conscious of their supervision practices and more aware of the options open to them for different modes of supervision, they will be able to reduce the student's emotional trauma. By extending compassionate action through recognising the vulnerabilities and pain of students, supervisors are in a position to model the type of conduct that should prevail in higher education. Doctoral pedagogies, as well as classroom pedagogies, cannot be devoid of caring relationships as made manifest in actions of compassion and empathy. When students are initiated into spaces and encounters of compassionate action, there is a better chance that they too will enact similar actions in relation to their potential students.

The point we are making is that student success at the doctoral level cannot just rely on notions of rationality, such as how well a student analyses arguments and how persuasive he or she articulates arguments in relation to doctoral writing and coherence. The doctoral journey is unique—not only because of its academic intensity but also because it foregrounds the strengths and weaknesses of students in relation to how well they are able to manage their stress, their time, their self-confidence and their maturity. As sets of soft skills, all of these speak to an emotional well-being, which is an invariable part of doctoral studies. In the main, especially concerning vulnerable students, the act of emotion—more specifically emotive judgement—should be considered equally important in any form of educational discourse. Next, we examine how compassionate action seems to extend democratic education.

Compassionate Action as an Extension of Democratic Education

Nussbaum (1996, 31) describes compassion as a painful emotion directed at another's misfortune or suffering that involves three beliefs: that the suffering is serious rather than trivial; that suffering is not caused primarily by the person's own culpable actions; and, that one is subject to a similar misfortune. Compassion, she continues, is an emotion directed at another person's suffering or lack of well-being. "It requires the thought that the other person is in a bad way, and a pretty seriously bad way" (Nussbaum 2003, 14). Nussbaum (2003, 14) notes that this assessment is made from the point of view of the person who experiences the emotion:

> It does not neglect the actual suffering of the other, which certainly should be estimated in taking the measure of the person's predicament. And yet it does not necessarily take at face value the estimate of the predicament this person will be able to form.

In the first place, when people engage publicly and democratically, they engage with one another on the basis of proffering intellectual reasons and emotive judgements. However, exercising the emotive judgement of compassion provokes in them "the ability to imagine the experiences of others and to participate in their sufferings" (Nussbaum 2001, 426). One would not be genuinely concerned about the well-being of others if there is no understanding of what others experience and when one actually extends empathy towards those who suffer. For example, postgraduate students in philosophy of education might not necessarily be cognitively equipped to offer plausible arguments for their judgements. They also find it challenging to see things beyond the text. In this way, these students struggle intellectually and invariably claim that they cannot make sense of theoretical constructions. They consequently find it overwhelmingly difficult to offer reconstructions and deconstructions of ideas and situations. In this way, teachers should not just teach them ways of persuasive argumentation but should also imagine the constraints students have to over come to do analytic philosophy of education. Consequently, such teachers would then act with compassion, and their emotive judgements would be geared towards understanding students' intellectual vulnerabilities. They (the university teachers) then proceed in a way to do something about the challenges students face in their learning. The point is, university teachers who apprehend students' intellectual vulnerabilities, act compassionately towards the students in doing something about remedying their cognitive challenges.

Secondly, when participants engage democratically in conversations about important matters that concern humanity, they begin to imagine the debilitating experiences of others on compassionate and—by implication—emotive grounds. As a result, they might then be encouraged "to notice the suffering of living creatures with a new keenness: the sight of blood, the death of animals, the distress of parents and friends, will become sources of disturbance" (Nussbaum 2001, 427). Such empathy will invariably result in good wishes towards those experiencing the suffering—that is, such persons invariably become "obsessed with the delineation of the possibilities and weaknesses of human life as such, and with the causes of the primary human difficulties ... as they construct the plights that human beings experience" (Nussbaum 2001, 429). Compassionate imagining attunes people to the sensitivities of human tragedy, and especially to becoming more compassionate towards those who "have suffered from the loathing and contempt of those in power" (Nussbaum 2001, 430). In this regard, it is necessary to listen to the stories and narratives of students.

By engaging with different lived experiences from different geographical locations and social realities, supervisors and teachers are able to enter (albeit imaginatively) the perspectives of their students. It is necessary and valuable to have some sense of where students come from, what their lives at home are like, what their motivations are for pursuing a doctorate, or for pursuing it a university far away from their home and, of course, what their aspirations are. A willingness to engage with students and to engage with them from their vantage points means that they become less strange to us as students, which, in turn, means that we, as supervisors, are more likely to respond to their vulnerabilities with compassion, care and empathy.

Thirdly, democratic human relations that inspire sentiments of compassion also promote relationships that are committed to a recognition of cultural pluralism. That is, compassionate concern for all humans should be extended to a recognition of diverse cultural ways of doing. However much we live with and for others, states Nussbaum (1992, 220), we are, each of us, "one in number", proceeding on a separate path through the world from birth to death. As such, each person feels only his or her own pain and not anyone else's. Nussbaum explains that because of separateness

> [E]ach human life has, so to speak, its own peculiar context and surroundings—objects, places, a history, particular friendships, locations, sexual ties—that are not exactly the same as those of anyone else, and in terms of which the person to some extent identifies oneself. (Nussbaum 1992, 220)

On the whole, Nussbaum (1992, 220) maintains that, "human beings recognize one another as beings who wish to have at least some separateness of context, a little space to move around in, some special items to love or use". For this reason, compassionate judgements should be about the promotion of human flourishing, which undermines any form of cultural relativism (Nussbaum 2001, 432). This implies that democratic relations should be about becoming participants in struggles against class, racial, national and ethnic superiority and should be about public deliberation that can protect cultural diversity. How does one show compassion towards those people against whom others might show prejudice? One has to be bold enough to demonstrate one's recognition of cultural diversity by acknowledging the fallibility of one's own cultural orientation. And, in doing so, one is always open to learn from other cultures and peoples. Acting compassionately implies that one restrains oneself from cultural relativism by recognising that faults may be found in one's own culture about which one remains open and reflective. As aptly stated by Nussbaum (2001, 359),

> All human beings are equal in worth, and we are fundamentally not members of families or cities, but *kosmopolitai*, members of the 'city-state of the universe'. This means that we should have equal concern for all; and that equal concern is incompatible with special attachments to kin.

We conclude this chapter by looking at how compassionate action and imagining hold the capacity to extend democratic justice, on the basis of human connectedness.

COMPASSIONATE DEMOCRATIC EDUCATION AS AN ENHANCEMENT OF DEMOCRATIC JUSTICE

Nussbaum (2000, 78–80) argues that each person is a worthy human being on the basis of the fact that everyone is able

- to imagine, think and reason—and to do these things in a truly human way;
- to form a conception of the good and to engage in critical reflection;
- to live with and towards others, to recognise and show concern for other human beings, to engage in various forms of social interaction—to be able to imagine the situation of another and to have compassion for that situation (and) to have the capability for both justice and friendship;
- to be treated as a dignified being (and as someone) whose worth is equal to that of others (which) entails, at a minimum, protection against discrimination on the basis of sex, race, sexual orientation, religion, caste, ethnicity or national origin;
- to work as a human being, exercising practical reason and entering into meaningful relationships of mutual recognition with others.

In sum, each person has the capability and potentiality to exercise reason, to express interest and concern for another and therefore to engage in a respectful interaction or relationship, which ultimately enhances practices of democratic citizenship.

To Nussbaum (1997), democratic citizenship education is constituted by compassionate imagining. Compassionate imagining involves "the ability to imagine what it is like to be in that [vulnerable] person's place … and also the ability to stand back and ask whether the person's own judgement has taken the full measure of what has happened" (Nussbaum 1997, 91). Consider, for example, students who spend long periods away from home, as they pursue doctoral studies, in the hope that such a qualification will not only afford them better lives, but also capacitate them to make a difference in their own communities and societies. These students are often vulnerable not only to financial constraints and loneliness but also to experiences of xenophobia, which—unfortunately—is common on South African campuses. As supervisors, we have to be able and willing to imagine what life must be like for these students, we have to be able to stand back from the expectations of thesis writing, so that we can see the vulnerability of the human in our presence. To imagine their vulnerability is to feel a humane connectedness, which enables us not only to act with compassion but also to enact democratic justice.

When students are taught to act with compassion, or when we, as supervisors, demonstrate that compassion through recognising the vulnerabilities of students, we begin to instil sensitivity to the pain of others. More importantly, in showing our sensitivity and empathy for the pain of others, we are prepared to act justly and with justice. To do so is to enhance our own sense of experience of the other to such an extent that we can imaginatively identify with the other. For Nussbaum (2002, 289), democratic citizenship education involves the cultivation of critical argumentation, reasoning and narrative imagination, that is, to imagine what it would be like to be in the position of someone different from oneself. For Nussbaum (2002, 292), the new emphasis on 'diversity' in universities is

[A way of] grappling with the altered requirements of citizenship in an era of global connection, an attempt to produce adults who can function as citizens not just of some local region or group but also, and more importantly, as citizens of a complex interlocking world—and function with a richness of human understanding and aspiration that cannot be supplied by economic connections alone.

Citizens who cultivate their humanity, "need, further, an ability to see themselves as not simply citizens of some local region or group but also, and above all, as human beings bound to all other human beings by ties of recognition and concern", according to Nussbaum (2002, 295).

Many students, like those described in this chapter, cannot exercise their basic human rights. Many of them come from war-ridden homes, intense poverty and very limited options of improving their lives and realising their capabilities. Human capabilities, according to Nussbaum (1999, 43), "exert a moral claim that they should be developed. Human beings are creatures such that, provided with the right educational and material support, they can become fully capable of the major human functions." Democratic justice implies that all humans, all students, regardless of their political, social or economic backgrounds, or their religious, cultural, ethnic or sexual orientation, be afforded the opportunities to develop and realise their capabilities. When we, as supervisors and teachers, neglect to take into account the vulnerabilities of our students, we fail to show compassion and we fail to enact justice. This is because, following Nussbaum (1997), compassion requires the recognition of a shared humanity and a shared humanity implies that justice is a shared right.

Summary

In this chapter, we analysed compassion as an emotive action in relation to democratic education—by paying specific attention to the student–supervisor relationship in relation to doctoral studies. We commenced by providing insights into the types of challenges doctoral students typically present during their studies, highlighting the reality that for many of them, the external constraints brought about through socio-economic constraints and political strife—both at home and in their host countries—often outweigh the internal demands of doctoral studies. For this reason, we argued that doctoral supervision cannot be limited to a reliance on constructions of rational argumentation and analyses, but necessarily involves emotive interactions seeped in capacities for compassionate action. Drawing on the seminal ideas of Martha Nussbaum, we showed, firstly, that compassion can be construed as an emotive judgement; secondly, acting compassionately is tantamount to recognising the vulnerabilities of others and doing something about changing unsatisfactory human conditions; and thirdly, compassionate action is about enhancing democratic relations among people that can cultivate human flourishing. We concluded that when we, as supervisors, exercise compassionate action, we ensure the realisation of democratic justice by recognising our shared humanity with our students.

References

Altbach, P. 2013. Advancing the National and Global Knowledge Economy: The Role of Research Universities in Developing Countries. *Studies in Higher Education* 38 (3): 316–330.

Grant, B.M. 2008. Agonistic Struggle: Master–Slave Dialogues in Humanities Supervision. *Arts and Humanities in Higher Education* 7 (1): 9–27.

Henderson, E.F. 2018. Anticipating Doctoral Supervision: (Not) Bridging the Transition from Supervisee to Supervisor. *Teaching in Higher Education* 23 (4): 403–418.

Nussbaum, M.C. 1992. Human Functioning and Social Justice: In Defense of Aristotelian Essentialism. *Political Theory* 20 (2): 202–246.

———. 1996. Compassion: The Basic Social Emotion. *Social Philosophy and Policy* 13: 27–58.

———. 1997. *Cultivating Humanity: A Classical Defence of Reform in Liberal Education*. Cambridge: Harvard University Press.

———. 1999. *Sex and Social Justice*. Oxford: Oxford University Press.

———. 2000. *Women and Human Development: The Capabilities Approach*. Cambridge: Cambridge University Press.

———. 2001. *Upheavals of Thought: The Intelligence of Emotions*. Cambridge: Cambridge University Press.

———. 2002. Education for Citizenship in an Era of Global Connection. *Studies in Philosophy and Education* 21 (4/5): 289–303.

———. 2003. Compassion and terror. *Daedalus* 132 (1): 10–26.

CHAPTER 6

Adab and Democratic Education

Abstract In this chapter, we proffer an argument for an interrelationship between the physical–intellectual and emotional dimensions of human life. In reference to the seminal thoughts of al-Attas, we argue that educational human encounters are constituted by the rational and the emotional dimensions of human action. Of pertinence to our non-bifurcationist view of knowledge, our contention is that human encounters about credible speech and respectful human conduct, have the potential to cultivate democratic human relations—referred to by al-Attas as actions grounded in *adab*. In the main, the point about democratic human encounters is that such encounters cannot be blind to the physical–intellectual and the emotional aspects of human life. Rather, as we argue, expressions of *adab*—that is, to act with refinement and decorum—can advance and enhance democratic encounters, through consciously averting disrespect and dismissiveness.

Keywords Human life • Human encounter • Non-bifurcation of knowledge • *Adab* (good action)

Introduction

As alluded to in Chap. 3, both of us have been reared as Muslims. And, as is typical within a South African context, both of us had particular sets of socialisation into public schooling, as dictated by a state curriculum on the one hand, and Muslim education, as promulgated through a madrassa system on the other. While separate in terms of content and form, these two systems of education are similar in terms of function and outcomes. However, it is important to note that the latter assessment might hold greater value and authenticity in a democratic South Africa than it did during apartheid South Africa, which was when we were both at school. Despite differences in curricular foci, and the underlying ideological disparities—one being public education through the propagation of Christian National Education and the other Muslim education—both systems were intent on producing a particular type of learner or pupil (in the case of public schooling) and Muslim (in the case of the madrassa). In other words, both systems of schooling were interested in socialising us with an adherence to and understanding of concepts pertaining to our learning. Our interest in this chapter, however, is in our madrassa education which, coupled with an initiation and socialisation into a particular body of religious knowledge and norms, emphasised *adab*.

Adab, loosely translated, as a concept and virtue, refers to good conduct or manners, through which all actions and interactions of Muslims ought to be governed. In other words, Muslims are required to display good conduct in every action—from eating, drinking, greeting and sleeping to how they engage in learning, business transactions and argumentation. To our understanding, therefore, *adab* is associated with good manners, for instance, politeness, mindfulness and kindness. Such an understanding of *adab* is not entirely incorrect, but it is somewhat parochial. In this chapter, by drawing on the ideas of Syed Muhammad Naquib al-Attas (1980), we are interested in offering an expansive analysis of *adab*, with a particular emphasis on considering it as a manifestation of democratic education.

Adab as Islamic Epistemology

As Halstead (2007, 283) explains, in Islam, there are three primary kinds of values: *akhlāq*, which refers to the duties and responsibilities set out in the shari'ah and in Islamic teaching generally; *adab*, which refers to the manners associated with good nurturing; and thirdly, the qualities of character possessed by a good Muslim, following the example of the Prophet Muhammad (the *Sunnah*). Loosely translated as 'ethics' or 'moral values', according to al-Qardawi (1981, cited in Halstead 2007), *akhlāq* can be classified into six categories, demonstrating the range of moral values expected in the life of the Muslim. These categories are *akhlāq* relating to self, to family, to society, to the animal world, to the physical environment and to the Creator. For Halstead (2007, 288), manners and etiquette extend the concept of morality beyond what is normally included in Western understandings of the term. He explains as follows:

> Because of the reverence in which the Prophet Muhammad is held in Islam, every small detail of his personal lifestyle and behaviour becomes a model for Muslims, including how he ate food and drank, how he prepared for bed, what side he slept on, how he washed, how he relieved himself, how he dyed his hair, how he responded to sneezing and yawning, how he acted in the presence of his wives. This is the main reason why the collections of hadith [prophetic sayings] are so important, because by providing a record of what the Prophet did and said, they simultaneously provide a guide to Muslims about how to behave. It is therefore rare to find any debate about family values or sexual values in Islam, because these matters are resolved by reference to the words and actions of the Prophet.

According to al-Attas (1980, 27), *adab* is the recognition and acknowledgement of the reality of knowledge that guides human judgement in relation to one's physical, intellectual and spiritual capacities and potentials, that is, education. Thus, to be an educated person is to demonstrate one's capacity to make judgements about this or that in relation to what one observes (the physical), thinks about (the intellectual) and that with which one connects emotionally (the spiritual). It is for this reason that al-Attas (1980, 27) premises his formulation of *adab* on a *hadith* or prophetic saying: *[a]ddabani rabbi fa-ahsana ta'dibi*—[m]y Lord educated me, and so made my education most excellent. To Kirabiev (2004, 100), *adab* embodies an "instantly recognizable orientation toward a certain way of life, a particular *modus operandi*, behavioral morality and ethics". On the one hand, this *adab*, as alluded to in the introduction to this chapter, is shaped and influenced by social interactions in the home, through rearing and interactions, and on the other, through madrassa education. Typically, madrassa curricula place a strong emphasis on the teaching and practices of *adab*—often treating it as a separate subject, constructed through particular historical accounts of the ways of being and acting of the Prophet Muhammad. In sum, generally, *adab* is considered not only the fulcrum of Muslim education, but as al-Attas (2005, 23) asserts, unless the acquisition of knowledge includes *adab*, it cannot be called education—defined by him as "right action that springs from self-discipline founded upon knowledge whose source is wisdom".

Normatively, Muslim education can be understood to be constituted and framed by three discernible, yet interrelated epistemological and ethical practices, namely socialisation (*tarbiyyah*), critical engagement (*ta'līm*) and social activism (*ta'dīb*). As such, firstly, when Muslims are socialised into the tenets and traditions in and about Islam, they are taught individually and socially to be the self in relation to others—in others words, that Islam is socially based. *Tarbiyyah*, explains Halstead (2004, 522), "comes from the Arabic (to grow, increase) and it refers to the development of individual potential and to the process of nurturing and guiding the child to a state of completeness". In turn, Saada (2018, 409) describes *tarbiyyah* as

> [Assisting Muslims] to feel connected to a transcendental power, which provides them answers to existential questions and the meaning of prayer, forgiveness, sacrifice, death, resurrection, and salvation, and thereby can successfully challenge the practices and public rhetoric of materialism, consumerism, and rationalism in modern life.

Tarbiyyah, he expounds, seeks to help Muslims achieve an inner peace by developing understandings and practices of love, kindness, compassion and selflessness. Secondly, critical engagement (*ta'līm*) for Muslims is associated with doing things in community, in other words, engaging in deliberation about matters in society that interest them. Halstead (2004, 522) clarifies that "*ta'līm* comes from the root 'alima (to know, be informed, perceive and discern) and refers to the imparting and receiving of knowledge, usually through training, instruction or other form of teaching". As such, *ta'līm* centres on thinking, reflecting on knowledge and practices and doing things in community, so that knowledge has a bearing on the interests of society. *Ta'līm*, explains Saada (2018, 409), is the process or the pedagogical methods of transmitting Islamic religious content and knowledge.

Thirdly, through social activism (*ta'dīb*), which underscores the basis of Muslim education, Muslims are taught that through belief, prayer, charity, fasting, pilgrimage and the exercise of morality, their actions ought to be responsive to societal demands. *Ta'dīb*, states Halstead (2004, 522), "comes from the root aduba (to be refined, disciplined, cultured) and refers to the process of character development and learning a sound basis for moral behaviour within the community and society at large". According to Saada (2018, 409), *ta'dib*, broadly speaking, refers to the process of disciplining the body and mind. It further refers to that aspect of Islamic philosophy requiring Muslim students to be familiar with the moral teachings of Islam and its ethical code, based primarily on the Qur'an, prophetic traditions known as *ahadith* and jurisprudence, known as the *fiqh*. According to Saada (2018, 409), the term *ta'dib* is derived from the word *adab*, which has connotations of courtesy, civility, etiquette and correct behaviour in both social and political contexts. Islam, continues Saada (2018, 409), provides considerable moral instructions on issues such as marriage and divorce, sexual relationships, trade, governance and treatment of the needy. As such, *ta'dib* and, hence, *adab* focus on civil rather than on spiritual transactions, as well as on Muslim duties towards fellow humans, society and the environment (Saada 2018). To Halstead (2007, 285), *adab* combines two different but related ways of understanding good behaviour—on the one hand, politeness, courtesy, etiquette, good upbringing, culture, refinement, good breeding and good manners, and on the other, morality and values.

The point about *adab*, more specifically, *ta'dib*, is that education cannot be construed without some understanding of what it means to live with and in relation to others. Having or displaying *adab* involves reflecting upon how one acts as an individual, as well as how one engages with others. Through an engagement with the physical realm, humans make sense of their encounters with society, humans and non-humans and the environment. And, making sense of human and non-human encounters in an intellectual way requires of one to do so under conditions of just actions. Whereas the liberal educationalist will discuss individual development in terms of the development of personal and moral autonomy, Halstead (2004, 522) explains that, in Islam, "it will be terms of the balanced growth of all sides of the individual's personality, spiritual and moral, leading to a higher level of religious understanding and commitment in all areas of life". It is for this reason that al-Attas (1980, 36–37) considers sciences of *fiqh, 'ilm, tawhid, tadhkir* and *hikmah* as conceptually linked to insight and discernment, knowledge of God and creation, knowledge of spiritual reality and truth, invocation and admonition, and wisdom, respectively, and constituted in an examination of the intellectual and spiritual realms of the human and non-human.

The point is, the aforementioned notion of *ta'dib* is inextricably intertwined with the pursuit of the physical, intellectual and spiritual dimensions of education. No longer is *adab* and *ta'dib* confined to *belles lettres* and professional and social etiquette (al-Attas 1980, 36). Rather, as Halstead (2004, 523) argues

> Education, like religion, can never be a purely individual affair; this is because individual development cannot take place without regard for the social environment in which it occurs, but more profoundly because education, in that it serves many individuals, is a means for making society what it is.

ADAB AS HUMAN CAPACITY AND POTENTIALITY

Central to *ta'dib* (education) is the position of humans in relation to the physical, intellectual and spiritual. Further, the pursuit of knowledge for Muslims—understood as those beings who claim an indebtedness towards God—is grounded in an examination of what is religious and philosophical. The point about showing an indebtedness towards God through the pursuit of a non-bifurcationist view of religious and philosophical is constituted in an understanding that education for humans is both religious and philosophical. This implies that to be educated is both a physical–intellectual and emotional pursuit of knowledge. Kirabiev (2004, 100), for example, compares *adab* to *paideia*, which he describes as a "total education", which includes notions of "general education" and "general cultures". The notion of *paideia*, he expounds has two basic meanings: the general culture of a cultivated human being, and basic education, which serves as an introduction to the highest stage of education (Kirabiev 2004).

Consequently, al-Attas (1980, 42) regards the study of

- the Qur'an (its recitation and interpretation);
- the *Sunnah* (the life of the Prophet Muhammad and messages of prophets before and the *ahadith* [authoritative sayings]);
- the *Shari'ah* (jurisprudence and law);
- theology or *tawhid*;
- metaphysics or *tasuwwuf* and linguistics (with reference to Arabic); and
- human sciences;

- natural sciences;
- applied sciences;
- technological sciences; as well as
- comparative and historical sciences, as intertwined and at the core of what it means to pursue an integrated approach to the pursuit of knowledge.

Put differently, humans cannot exclusively embark on the physical intellectual, independent of the spiritual or emotional. "No single branch of knowledge ought to be pursued indefinitely exclusively of others, for that would result in disharmony, which would affect the unity of knowledge, and render its validity questionable" (al-Attas 1980, 44).

Thus, from the aforementioned, it is evident that *ta'dib* (education) is constituted by physical–intellectual and emotional dimensions of human encounters and knowledge. If *ta'dib* is not evident in society—or more specifically educational institutions—then the educational practices of humans would be devoid of *adab* and, by implication, would result in human actions in which there would be "confusion and error in knowledge … [that] creates the condition which enables false leaders in all spheres of life to emerge and thrive, causing the condition of injustice (*zulm*)" (al-Attas 1980, 34). Our understanding of al-Attas's admonition that "false leaders" (al-Attas 1980, 34) will emerge is tantamount to saying that undemocratic human encounters would dominate, whereby people who lack the intellectual–emotional aspects of what it means to engage in encounters will seemingly control and dominate societal matters. This is so, on the grounds that democratic encounters are supposedly meant to provoke just and defensible understandings of human events in the world. And, if the latter is not possible, it could only be as a corollary of the dominance of humans who miss the point of the non-separation of knowledge—that is, such humans attempt to make plausible judgements of worldly affairs without drawing on both the physical–intellectual and emotional dimensions of knowledge and society. Al-Attas (1980, 35) posits that, when the latter happens, it could only be as a consequence of a loss of *adab*, which "means the loss of the capacity for discernment of the right and proper places of things".

Of course, humans have the capacity to embark on physical–intellectual and emotional pursuits of knowledge. However, there is always the possibility that their efforts might be constrained. And, as we have argued earlier, one way of impeding their educational encounters would be to embark on a bifurcationist pursuit of knowledge. Such an idea of knowledge (re)construction and/or deconstruction is perhaps not possible if one were to come up with defensible and just understandings of concepts and practices. If the latter is not possible, the potential for injustice to prevail in human encounters would be highly likely. Moreover, if human encounters, following al-Attas's idea of *ta'dib* (education) were to be just and democratic, the potentiality should always be there for encounters to be situated in a non-bifurcationist understanding of the physical–intellectual and the emotional dimensions of educative human activity. If the latter were to be present, the potential would remain for human encounters to be guided by insight and discernment, and even the possibility to see things anew—that is, democratic education would enframe such human encounters.

What intrigues us about the concept of *ta'dib* (education) as espoused by al-Attas is not only that the physical–intellectual and emotional aspects of educational activity are advanced, but more poignantly, that a particular human being is being reified. For al-Attas (1980, vi) the notion of *ta'dib* (education) for a Muslim (one indebted to God) is about producing a good person. For al-Attas, a good person is one which acts with justice in whatever he or she does. In his words, "[t]he external manifestation of justice in life and society is none other than the occurrence within it of *adab*" (al-Attas 1993, 149). And, persons of *adab* are those who have been invited to participate in a banquet, which implies that those engaged in *adab* treat one another with "honor and prestige ... in speech, conduct and etiquette" (al-Attas 1993, 149). First, to be honourable in speech implies that one inclines oneself to listening to others. That is, one respects the speech of others and before responding, one thinks through what one has heard. In turn, one interprets and responds to others' speech because one has something worthwhile to say about what one has heard—this means one talks back to the words of others. Second, one conducts oneself in such a way that one is persuaded by reasons. And, if one finds someone else's reasons unconvincing it is prudent that one justifies why one disagrees with someone or finds his or her speech injudicious. That is, one does not leave the conversation just because one disagrees with someone else's views. Thirdly, showing good etiquette implies that one can be provocative, for instance by eliciting more persuasive responses, but one does not insult and humiliate others just because one finds others' views ill conceived.

Following the above, displaying *adab* in day-to-day, uncontested interactions is, of course, much easier than in moments of disagreement and controversy. Yet, it is precisely in moments of debates and dissensus that *adab* is most necessary and ought to be the foundational basis of engagement. This is especially pertinent in contexts of diametrically opposed worldviews or beliefs where, without *adab* or mindful engagement, respectful dialogue and ways of acting will not flourish. That an individual, for example, holds a view that hate speech should not be disallowed in a liberal democracy, does not necessarily imply that he or she is in the business of spewing out hate speech or that he or she is a hateful person. Concomitantly, it cannot be assumed that those who are opposed to hate speech in a liberal society are necessarily opposed to free speech. Both these viewpoints have their own merits and should be afforded equal weighting through courtesies of listening and attentiveness. What concerns and shapes *adab* is a need to find a consistent departure point of respect for others, and views that might be entirely opposite and antagonistic to one's own. In this sense, one of the ways in which to understand *adab* is that an action which attempts to avert what might be interpreted as speech and actions of hostility and alienation. In this sense, *adab* is intent upon sustaining the conditions necessary for sincere and respectful engagement.

Summary

In this chapter, we made an argument for an interrelationship between the physical–intellectual and emotional dimensions of human life. In reference to the seminal thoughts of al-Attas, we have found that educational human encounters are constituted by the rational and the emotional dimensions of human action. Of pertinence to our non-bifurcationist view of knowledge, our contention is that human encounters about credible speech and respectful human conduct have the potential to cultivate democratic human relations—referred to by al-Attas as actions grounded in *adab*. In the main, the point about democratic human encounters is that such encounters cannot be blind to the physical–intellectual and the emotional aspects of human life. Rather, as we have argued, expressions of *adab*— that is, to act with refinement and decorum—could advance and enhance democratic encounters, through consciously averting disrespect and dismissiveness.

REFERENCES

Al-Attas, S.M.N. 1980. *The Concept of Education in Islam: A Framework for an Islamic Philosophy of Education*. Kuala Lumpur: International Institute of Islamic Thought and Civilisation Publications.

———. 1993. *Islam and Secularism*. Kuala Lumpur: International Institute of Islamic Thought and Civilisation Publications.

———. 2005. Islam and Secularism. *Journal of Islamic Philosophy* 1: 11–43.

Al-Qardawi, Y. 1981. *Al-Khasā'is al-'ammah lil Islāmi [The Universal Characteristics of Islam]*. Qaherah: Maktabah Wahbah.

Halstead, J.M. 2004. An Islamic Concept of Education. *Comparative Education* 40 (4): 517–530.

———. 2007. Islamic Values: A Distinctive Framework for Moral Education? *Journal of Moral Education* 36 (3): 283–296.

Kirabiev, N. 2004. Paideia and *Adab* in Islam. In *Educating for Democracy: Paideia in an Age of Uncertainty*, ed. A.M. Olson, D.M. Steiner, and I.S. Tuuli, 97–102. New York: Rowan & Littlefield.

Saada, N. 2018. The Theology of Islamic Education from Salafi and Liberal Perspectives. *Religious Education* 113 (4): 406–418.

CHAPTER 7

Ibn al-Arabi's Idea of *Al-insan Al-kamil* (the Perfect Human) and Democratic Education

Abstract In this chapter, we draw on some of the seminal ideas of Ibn al-Arabi, who is arguably one of the most influential and intellectual philosophers in Islamic philosophy. In drawing on his depiction of the 'perfect man' or the 'perfect human', we show that it is through the imagination that human beings might come to know God, and hence, come to self-realisation. Coming to self-realisation implies that human beings take account of their own *haqq* [right and proper action], and of their *haqq* in relation to others. The 'perfect human', therefore, assumes responsibility for himself, his actions and his intuitive connection with God. Following this discussion we examine the implications and enhancement of the 'perfect human' to and for democratic education.

Keywords Perfect human • Imagination • Rightful action • Democratic education

INTRODUCTION

Al-Attas's seminal thoughts as espoused in the previous chapter, in particular his ideas pertaining to *ta'dib* (education), can be categorised among the phenomenal contributions of Sufis—that is, those intellectuals who regard themselves as having enhanced the tradition of Islamic thought and civilisation in relation to *tasawwuf* (Islamic metaphysics). As Weisman

(2001, 62) explains, Sufism does not imply that the world does not exist at all, "but only that in reality the world is different from how the common people perceive it to be, since its appearance is creation and its essence is God". The world, therefore, "is like the imagination that every intelligent being finds within himself". In this chapter, we examine a concept widely referred to as *al-insan al-kamil* (the perfect human being) within Islamic metaphysics with reference to the thoughts of one of Islam's leading Sufi scholars, namely the Andalusian-born scholar, Muhammad ibn 'Ali ibn al-Arabi (1165 AD), better known as Muhyiddin (the Revivifier of Religion). Although Western scholarship and much of the later Islamic tradition classify Ibn al-Arabi as a 'Sufi', Chittick (2008) is of the view that Ibn al-Arabi's works cover the whole gamut of Islamic sciences, including Qur'anic commentary, *ahadith* (the lived example of the Prophet Muhammad), jurisprudence, principles of jurisprudence, theology, philosophy and mysticism.

THE PERFECT HUMAN

Ibn al-Arabi (1988), in his *al-Futuhat al-Makkiyyah*, elucidates the notion that human agency is shared by both God and human, and the latter ought to strive towards perfection. He describes the idea of the 'perfect man' (*insan al-kamil*) as a responsible human being who through rational thinking and spiritual insight devotes him- or herself to Allah, humanity and the environment. Ultimately, the evolution and potentiality of the 'perfect man' centres on the relationship between an individual and his or her Lord. Weisman (2001, 61) argues that, at the centre of Ibn al-Arabi's teachings is the concept of *wahdat al-wujud*, or the 'unity of being'—in which "both God and His creation (*al-Haqq wal-khalq*), the internal things in the external and the external things in the internal, without each being concealed from the other". Chittick (2008) however points out that it is important to note that Ibn al-Arabi never actually used the expression *wahdat al-wujud*. Ibn al-Arabi emphasised the concept of *tawhid* (oneness) or 'unity of finding'—as in 'finding' God (Chittick 1989)—as his guiding principle, and it was unequivocal to him that there is no other Being, but God, and that everything other than God is unreal (Chittick 2008).

Weisman (2001, 61) explains that knowing God (*ma'rifa*) means to perceive reality from a combination of the two perspectives of the divine and the earthly (or physical). As such, the principle of *wahdat al-wujud* gives rise to a concept of a mutual relationship between God and his creatures (Weisman 2001). Weisman (2001, 61) continues by remarking that Ibn al-Arabi maintained that human beings and God are mutually dependent. "Just as we need God to realise our prototypes (*wujud al-a'yan al-thabita*) so He needs us to make manifest His manifestations (*zuhur mazahirihi*)." Despite this dependency, "this existential mutuality is entirely vested in God, the only One who really exists" (Weisman 2001, 61).

According to Chittick (2008), Ibn al-Arabi sees the human soul as an unlimited potential and understands the goal of life to lie in the actualisation of that potential. However, Ibn al-Arabi is adamant that "[i]magination is the widest known thing" because "it exercises its properties through its reality over every thing and non-thing. It gives form to absolute non-existence, the impossible, the Necessary, and possibility; it makes existence nonexistent and nonexistence existent" (Ibn 'Arabî, *al-Futûhât* 1911, cited in Chittick 2008). Chittick (2008) explains that, as the model of human possibility, the 'perfect man', or 'perfect human' "represents the individual who has traversed the circle of existence"—he has returned to his origin. The 'perfect human' "is the spirit that animates the cosmos". As Chittick (2006, 131) further points out, to Ibn al-Arabi, the cosmos can have no final boundaries, for God is eternally the Creator. It therefore follows that human beings' knowledge of the cosmos, like their knowledge of their Creator, can have no final limit, and knowledge of the universe is itself knowledge of God (Chittick 2006). The point is not that human beings should become one with God; rather, they should come to know God and themselves and the world in which they find themselves. Following Ibn al-Arabi, it is through the imagination that human beings might come to know God, and hence come to self-realisation. Once this occurs, then they would have reached the state of the 'perfect human', and the purpose of creation would have been fulfilled.

In an exposition of al-Arabi's idea of the perfect human, Abid Nayif Diyab (2000, 34) avers that such an idea is based on the presupposition that everything, including human development, is constitutive of "the perfect manifestation of Deity (God) and therefore it cannot be bad or deficient". However, according to Ibn al-Arabi (1988), although God predestines human acts, and humans are a manifestation of God (such as God predicting human actions), His knowledge of things and events—His Omniscience—does not constrain the exercise of human free will. As aptly stated by Diyab (2000, 31),

Man [being human] can now be seen as a manifestation of God, but simultaneously independent, containing within himself the sources of his own actions in future life. God foresees how every self is going to behave, but neither this foreknowledge nor His Will changes the inherent tendencies and motives of one's self.

At least three ideas emanate from Ibn al-Arabi's notion of 'the perfect human'. Firstly, humans are responsible for their own actions, and their intuitive connection with God is a manifestation of their actuality and potentiality to do good as becoming beings. Hence, the dictum "whoever knows himself [or herself], knows his [or her] Lord—*man arafa nafsahu qad arafa rabbahu*" (Diyab 2000, 40). Secondly, when humans err, their ill-conceived judgements, obviously known to God, should not be deemed God's responsibility, as they (humans) have the capability to resist errors of judgement. Ibn al-Arabi (1988) recognises humans' disposition to commit wrongs freely, but also affirms humans' responsibility to assume answerability for their own dereliction. Thirdly, Ibn al-Arabi's idea of 'the perfect human' further brings into consideration that the idea of eschatology should also be rethought. If the idea of 'the perfect human' is what is central to Ibn al-Arabi's metaphysics, then the notions of paradise (*jannah*) and hell (*jahannam*) should be understood in the light of human perfection. This implies that the destiny of humans cannot be assigned to a permanent torment of hell. In other words, even those in hell would be subjected to the possibilities of angelic, prophetic and saintly intercession to release them from hell to join a paradise of knowledge and revelation. In other words, "those ... in Hell, will through their own disposition, find it their fitting exile, and regard all other abodes harmful to them ... so that this exile of sinners will become a happy paradise, but after the expiration of the periods of punishment" (Diyab 2000, 41). The point is, being in hell is considered a temporary abode for sinners and their final destination of perfect humans will be paradise in which they would be relieved from suffering.

Next, we examine the implications of such an idea of 'the perfect human' for the practice of democratic education.

DEMOCRATIC EDUCATION AKIN TO 'THE PERFECT HUMAN'

Following on the above discussion, it becomes apparent that for Ibn al-Arabi, knowledge or *'ilm* is key to knowing God, and hence, knowing oneself. For Ibn al-Arabi, there is no goal beyond knowledge (Chittick

2006). Chittick (1989, 3) explains that, for Ibn al-Arabi, it is imperative for human beings to ask, "How can I find God?" Having answered this question, Chittick (1989, 3) continues, "they must then set to verify the truth of their answer by finding God in fact, not in theory. Once they have verified the truth, they have passed beyond the veils, which exist between them and God, and stand in his presence" (Chittick 1989). Chittick (1989, 3) explains that, to find God, is to be lost and found simultaneously, it is knowing and not knowing, affirming and negating. The difference between the 'Finders'—those who have found God—and those who have not, is that the 'Finders' are fully aware of their ambiguous situation (Chittick 1989, 4).

For this reason, human beings are only able to actualise their potential when they arrive at knowledge of the self. A conception of self-knowledge, alongside a recognition of a 'unity of being', has profound implications for democratic education. Knowing oneself, as maintained by Ibn al-Arabi, implies that the external conditions of one's existence should not deter or detract one from knowing God, oneself as well as others for the simple reason that there is 'unity of being'.

At this point, it becomes necessary to take account of the absolute centrality of knowledge—that is, the way in which human beings might come to know God, themselves and others. Ibn al-Arabi distinguishes between knowledge that is beneficial, and that which is not. In short, explains Chittick (2006, 138), "beneficial knowledge is knowledge of the what and the why of ourselves and of things". In order to know a thing truly and to benefit from the knowledge, he continues, we need to know what it is, and we need to know how we should respond to it. True knowledge of things is not 'acquired' or gained by learning, but rather, it is gained "by presence with God" (Chittick 2006, 128–129).

> Knowledge of the cosmos, however, can also be the greatest veil on the path to God, because the more man focuses on signs and marks without recognizing what they signify, the more he is overcome by the darkness that prevents him from seeing things as they are. From this point of view, any knowledge of the universe that does not recognize the divine workings and acknowledge the signs of God for what they are does not deserve the name 'knowledge'. Rather, it is a diversion, a veil, and an ignorance dressed as knowledge. (Chittick 2006, 131)

Furthermore, whatever human beings come to know is always and only known in relation to other things, or in relation to God. Ibn al-Arabi avers that only God "has direct, unmediated knowledge of Himself and of things in themselves" (Chittick 2006, 132). In the light of Ibn al-Arabi's contention that there is no separation or barrier between God (as divine) and humans (as earthly beings), and in the light of his focus on the delimitations of the imagination, knowledge cannot be understood only in terms of rational reasoning. This is because "[e]very knowledge gained through reason or any other created mode of knowing is defined and constricted by the limitations of everything other than God. Man can understand things only inasmuch as his native ability, circumstances, upbringing, and training allows him to" (Chittick 2006, 132). In putting complete faith in reasons, Chittick (1989, ix) asserts that, "the West forgot that imagination opens up the soul to certain possibilities of perceiving and understanding not available to the rational mind". As such, knowledge is not only transmitted and shared through reasoning, but can also unfold through revelation (*wahy*), as well as through intuition—that is, through instinctive and perceptual experiences of God, oneself and others. To this end, human beings cannot be separated by that which is an external, because knowledge of self and others already exists within the unity of being human. According to Chittick (2008, ix), in Qur'anic terms:

> [T]he locus of awareness and consciousness is the heart (*qalb*), a word that has the verbal sense of fluctuation and transmutation (*taqallub*). According to Ibn 'Arabî, the heart has two eyes, reason and imagination, and the dominance of either distorts perception and awareness. The rational path of philosophers and theologians needs to be complemented by the mystical intuition of the Sufis, the 'unveiling' (*kashf*) that allows for imaginal—not 'imaginary'—vision. The heart, which in itself is unitary consciousness, must become attuned to its own fluctuation, at one beat seeing God's incomparability with the eye of reason, at the next seeing his similarity with the eye of imagination.

What, therefore, are the implications of aspiring towards becoming the 'perfect human' for democratic education? Specifically, what does it mean for the enhancement of democratic ways of being and acting, if humans were to engage with others in an understanding of a unity of being and imagination? For Ibn al-Arabi, the answer resides in how human beings understand themselves, and how they understand themselves in relation to others. Ibn al-Arabi maintains that inasmuch as each human being has a *haqq*—that is "truth and true, reality and real, propriety and proper, appropriateness and appropriate, rightness and right"—each human being has a *haqq* pertaining to them (Chittick 2006, 135–138). This implies, according to Chittick (2006, 138), that all human beings have "a proper situation", and a "correct mode of being", and as human beings, who exist as a unity of being, we are responsible for affording all others their *haqq*—that is, right, real, proper and appropriate action.

Following on the above, when humans engage in democratic education, they firstly assume responsibility for their speech and actions—that is, they recognise and accept their *haqq* in relation to others. It is not as if human beings are merely coerced into saying and doing this or that; they realise that others have the right to be treated in a proper and right way. That is, they assume responsibility for their own actions and recognise that their democratic practices remain in becoming. This implies that there cannot be conclusiveness about educational matters, for that in itself would be the end of education. Human beings remain open and reflective about that which is still to come together with looking introspectively at their own practices—all the while being mindful of themselves and their proper responsibility in relation to others.

Secondly, humans engaged in democratic education do not fear making mistakes as their errors in judgement are forms of learning to come up with more plausible perspectives about education. This is because, as Ibn al-Arabi argues, human beings can know things only in the measure of themselves; they cannot know everything, and ultimately, they can only know themselves (Chittick 2006, 132). It is, therefore, expected that, as human beings aspire towards becoming the 'perfect human', they will err and stumble. And, as previously stated, inasmuch as Ibn al-Arabi (1988) recognises humans' disposition to commit wrongs freely, he also affirms humans' responsibility to assume answerability for their own dereliction. In this way, misreadings and slip-ups are perceived as expedient to reach justifiable conclusions without being perturbed about always getting things right.

Thirdly, humans' quest to be 'perfect' beings when they engage in democratic educational practices should be geared towards consistent and moderate efforts to reach thoughtful and prudent judgements and to remain open to the possibility that things might be seen otherwise. Misunderstandings and misconceptions should be considered epistemological platforms for deliberating in and about more cogent and compelling truth claims. The democratic engagement will last as long as humans remain attuned to the possibility that things would not have to be the same and that errors in judgement should be used to contrive more tenable claims. To Ibn al-Arabi, the soul, like knowledge, is like an ocean without a shore (Chittick 2006), which means that the potentiality for other ways of knowing and being is always within reach. To this end, as long as human beings are in search of 'finding' God, and hence, themselves, they engage in deliberative actions of knowing and not knowing.

Summary

In this chapter, we have drawn on some of the seminal ideas of Ibn al-Arabi, who is arguably one of the most influential intellectuals in Islamic philosophy. In drawing on his depiction of the 'perfect man' or the 'perfect human', we have shown that it is through the imagination that human beings might come to know God, and hence, come to self-realisation. Coming to self-realisation implies that human beings take account of their own *haqq* (right and proper action) and of their *haqq* in relation to others. The 'perfect human', therefore, assumes responsibility for him- or herself, his (or her) actions and his (or her) intuitive connection with God. Following this discussion, we turned our attention to the implications and enhancement of the 'perfect human' to and for democratic education. In this regard, we paid particular attention to Ibn al-Arabi's conceptions of knowledge—as in 'finding' or coming into the presence of God—and *haqq*—truthful, right and appropriate action. In sum, we argued that democratic education constituted by a notion of the 'perfect human' takes responsibility to engage deliberatively and to hold one another answerable to the comings of the association. Moreover, to remain committed to the democratic engagement is to be engaged in enhancing judgements continually, thus sharpening discernments. Finally, a democratic education geared towards the cultivation of the 'perfect human'—an idea that remains in potentiality—is always in becoming without any conclusiveness about it.

References

Chittick, W.C. 1989. *The Sufi Path of Knowledge: Ibn al-Arabi's Metaphysics of Imagination*. Albany, NY: State University of New York Press.
———. 2006. Ibn 'Arabī on the Benefit of Knowledge. In *The Essential Sophia: The Journal of Traditional Studies*, ed. S.H. Nasr and K. O'Brien, 126–143. Bloomington, IN: World Wisdom.

———. 2008. Ibn Arabi. In *The Stanford Encyclopedia of Philosophy*, ed. E.N. Zalta, Summer 2018 ed. https://plato.stanford.edu/archives/sum2018/entries/ibn-arabi. Accessed 10 Apr 2019.

Diyab, A.N. 2000. Ibn Arabi on Human Freedom, Destiny and the Problem of Evil. *Al-Shajarah – Journal of the International Institute of Islamic Thought and Civilization* 5 (1): 25–43.

Ibn al-Arabi, M. 1988. *Al-Futuhat al-Makkiyah*. New ed. Ed. U.Y. Al-Majlis al-Ala li al-Thaqafah. Beirut: Dar al-Fikr.

Weisman, I. 2001. God and the Perfect Man in the Experience of Abd al-Qadir al-Jaza'iri. *Journal of the Muhyiddin Ibn' Arabi Society* 30: 55–72.

CHAPTER 8

Ibn Sina's Notion of Intuition and Claims of Democratic Education

Abstract In this chapter, we elucidate Ibn Sina's notion of intuition (*hads*) in relation to practices that are rational, imaginative and perceptive. We explain his conceptions of knowledge and intuition [*hads*]—highlighting that to Ibn Sina, human beings do not only come into this world without any innate knowledge but, indeed, have the potentiality to come to their own ways of seeing themselves, others and the world around them, through their own experiences. By implication, human intuitive intelligence is constituted by both rational and emotive aspects. And, when humans engage in democratic educational practices, their deliberations should be underscored by both cognitive and emotive dimensions of knowing, acting and being.

Keywords Intuition • Rationality • Imagination • Perception • Emotion

INTRODUCTION

Abu 'Ali al-Husayn ibn Sina (*c.* 980–1037)—better known as Avicenna—was born in Afshana near Bukhara in Central Asia. Most appropriately known as a polymath and physician, he is renowned for his metaphysics of being, concerned with understanding the existence of the human self vis-à-vis its contingency. His theories of the soul, intellect and cosmos, coupled with his non-bifurcationist view of religion and philosophy—that is, religion is as philosophical as philosophy is religious—provoked him to proffer noteworthy contributions in relation to a theory of being. It may be said, states Fazlur Rahman (1963, 497), that Ibn Sina was a citizen of two intellectual-spiritual worlds: the Hellenic and the Islamic. In his own mind, Rahman (1963, 497) asserts, Ibn Sin had so intrinsically unified the two worlds that they were identical; the question of disloyalty to either, therefore, did not arise for him at all.

> Under this circumstance, both traditional Islam and the heritage of Hellenism were inevitably interpreted and modified to a greater or lesser extent. This is apparent in the whole of his philosophy which enters into the technically religious field, but is most palpably so in his doctrine of prophecy. (Rahman 1963, 497)

In this chapter, it is Ibn Sina's pronouncements on being and knowledge underscored by a conception of intuition that draw us to his rational-cum-emotive notion of education.

Ibn Sina's Theory of Knowledge

Rahman (1963, 491) states that, in accordance with the universal Greek tradition, Ibn Sina described all knowledge as some sort of abstraction on the part of the cognisant of the form of the thing known. His chief emphasis was on the degrees of this abstracting power in different cognitive faculties. Hence, explains Rahman (1963, 491)

> [S]ense-perception needs the very presence of matter for its cognitive act; imagination is free from the presence of actual matter but cannot cognize without material attachments and accidents which give to the image its particularity, whereas in intellect alone the pure form is cognized in its universality.

Ibn Sina's theory of knowledge is based on four faculties: sense perception, retention, imagination and estimation. In contrast to the theory of innatism, which holds that the mind is born already in possession of certain knowledge, Ibn Sina maintained that at birth, the human intellect is a *tabula rasa*—"a pure potentiality that is actualised through education and comes to know". As a posteriori approach (an empirical approach to knowledge), an individual comes to know what he or she knows by acquiring empirical familiarity with various objects in this world. Rahman (1963, 494) explains the theory or doctrine of *tabula rasa* as follows:

> The doctrine, in brief, distinguishes between a potential intellect in man and an active intellect outside man, through the influence and guidance of which the former develops and matures. Basically, the problem is that of the origin of human cognition and it is explained on the assumption of a supra-human transcendent intellect which, when the human intellect is ready, bestows knowledge upon it ... Ibn Sina holds that the potential intellect in man is an indivisible, immaterial, and indestructible substance although it is generated at a definite time and as something personal to each individual.

Notions of the *tabula rasa* theory are evident in Aristotle's (1931) *De Anima*—"What [the mind] thinks must be in it just as characters may be said to be on a writing tablet (grammateion) on which as yet nothing actually stands written" (1931, 430a). And, of course, in John Locke's, *An Essay Concerning Human Understanding* (written in 1689). Like Ibn Sina, Locke (1997) posits that the human mind is a *tabula rasa*, a 'blank tablet' or a 'white paper'. To Locke (1997), the only knowledge, which humans can have, is a posteriori—in other words, knowledge based upon experience. As explained by Duschinsky (2012, 515), Locke suggests that, "the tabula rasa is not an image of cognitive formlessness, but of a state that requires correct instruction in order to form representations of true moral principles".

Knowledge, following Ibn Sina, is developed through a syllogistic method of reasoning; observations lead to prepositional statements, which when compounded, lead to further abstract concepts. The intellect itself possesses levels of development: from the material intellect (*al-'aql al-hayulani*)—the potentiality that can acquire knowledge—to the active intellect (*al-'aql al-fa'il*)—the state of the human intellect at conjunction with the perfect source of knowledge (Nazari 2015).

Ibn Sina and Intuition of Being

Sense perception itself is the basis for knowledge by definition (Aminrazavi 2003, 204). Aminrazavi (2003, 206) continues by saying Ibn Sina realises the need "for a pre-cognitive ability that is based on a priori concepts and serves as the fundamental epistemic ground". One of the many arguments

Ibn Sina offers in this regard, according to Aminrazavi (2003, 206), is his ontological argument for the existence of God

> He maintains that since God is incorporeal, God cannot be known by the senses and that, therefore, either God cannot be known or God can only be known through some other way. He then argues that since we know God, it follows that empiricism fails and rationalism or mysticism may be the only other available alternative.

To Ibn Sina, human beings and animals perceive particulars by means of sense, and human beings acquire knowledge of universals through reason (Kabadayi 2006). Kabadayi (2006, 21) explains that the rational soul of human beings is conscious of its own faculty, not with the help of an external bodily sense, but immediately by the exercise of its own reasoning power—that is, its intuition. Moreover, following Ibn Sina, it is in the exercise of its own reasoning power that the soul achieves perfection of knowledge and attains knowledge of itself. The soul, therefore, as explained by Kabadayi (2006, 21), is not a dependent entity, despite the fact that it is connected with the body and receives sensations by means of it. Ibn Sina treats the soul as a collection of faculties or forces which act on the body. He sees the soul as "a substance and [...] not a form of the body to which it is attached intimately by some kind of mystical relation between the two" (Rahman 1963, 487). Rahman (1963, 487) provides the following elaboration:

> There is in the soul which emerges from the separate substance of the active intelligence simultaneously with the emergence of a body with a definite temperament, a definite inclination to attach itself to this body, to care for it, and direct it to the mutual benefit. Further, the soul, as being incorporeal, is a simple substance and this ensures for it indestructibility and survival, after its origination, even when its body is destroyed. But if at the transcendental level the soul is a pure spiritual entity and the body does not enter into its definition even as a relational concept, at the phenomenal level the body must be included in its definition as a building enters into the definition of a (definite) builder. That is why Ibn Sina says that the study of the phenomenal aspect of the soul is in the field of natural science, while its transcendental being belongs to the study of metaphysics.

According to Syamsuddin Arif (2000, 94–95), the term Ibn Sina primarily used for intuition is *hads* or an act of acuteness of mind and soul, such as when one is divinely inspired. In addition, Arif (2000, 99) avers that, intuition can also be couched in relation to *'aql* (reason), *fitrah* (innate faculty), *quwaat al-nafs* (mental aptitude). According to Eran (2007, 40), the particular qualities of *hads* are the ability to arrive at a conclusion instantaneously and the ability to arrive at a conclusion or truth with no external aid and without prior learning. Eran (2007, 40) adds that Ibn Sina "succeeds in grounding his theory in a natural base by arguing that the special power of hads varies in quantity, frequency and quality in different individuals". In other words, inasmuch as *hads* can be found abundantly in some individuals, it does not exist in other individuals at all. Examining the notion of *hads* (intuition) in relation to metaphysics, Ibn Sina offers two ways of arriving at knowledge: *istish'ar* (intuitive knowledge) and *qiyas* (syllogistic reasoning), both constituting *hads* (intuition) (Arif 2000, 125). By implication, *hads* (intuition) comprises both rational and emotive dimensions. In his *Shifa Tabiyyat al-Nafs*, Ibn Sina (1975, 219–220) relates *hads* (intuition) to notions of *tahkayyal* (imagine) and *tawahham* (surmise), *shu'ur* (intellectual perception) and *'aql* (rational cognition).

Marmura (1991, 336) describes two types of intuition: in its strongest form, he refers to *al-hads al-baligh*, which comes about without its object being sought after and without reflection. He also refers to lesser forms of intuition, where the intelligible is sought and attained with difficulty, after reflection. Sometimes, continues Marmura (1991, 336), "reflection fails to bring about the intuition immediately and sometimes individuals give up on it, so to speak, to have it unexpectedly occur to them". Ideally, however, "reflection is akin to receiving an unsolicited gift" (Marmura 1991, 336).

What is unclear for Marmura (1991, 341) is whether intuition (*hads*) is intuitive knowledge (*ma'rifa*) or knowledge in a broad sense (*'ilm*). Marmura (1991, 341) contends that it is possible to conceive of *hads* as either descriptive or prescriptive. The latter is concerned with action and, hence, the commands or prohibitions of the law. Descriptive knowledge, on the other hand, is basically metaphysical, claiming to be demonstrative and includes the intuition of middle terms—"It is hence not the direct experiencing of entities, but knowledge of concepts and propositions, of intelligibles, primary and secondary" (Marmura 1991, 341). Sari Nuseibeh's (2002, 837) account of Ibn Sinian epistemology describes *ma'rifah* as that way of knowing that "once the human intellect reaches this point it would not be impossible to start perceiving images of particulars ... from the future". That is, *ma'rifah* is a form of intuitive cognition that allows an individual to think of alternative futures. Bringing the latter idea of *ma'rifah* into conversation with democratic education, it cannot be that such a form of education should only be concerned with the present. Rather, democratic education is also about taking imaginative risks towards a future that remains in becoming. Such a future would be about situating the self-consciousness of an individual, who endeavours to imagine unforeseen democratic possibilities.

From Ibn Sina's depiction of intuition (*hads*) it can be deferred that the practice has a rational, imaginative and perceptive perspective. In this sense, human intuitive intelligence has both an intellectual and an emotive aspect. It is in the latter regard that we concur with Arif's (2000, 121) assertion that Ibn Sina's unity of self-consciousness is premised on the notion that "our very awareness of ourselves is constantly present, intuitively clear". To Ibn Sina, an individual's self-consciousness is a continuous stream whose beginning and end are unknown (Aminrazavi 2003, 208). Aminrazavi (2003, 208) explains that Ibn Sina distinguishes between two cognitive (self-consciousness) processes with regard to the knowledge of the self: "consciousness in itself" and "consciousness through consciousness". According to Aminrazavi (2003, 208):

> Ibn Sina tells us that the fact that I perceive myself as myself is verifiable neither by outsiders nor by myself. How do I know that I am who I think I am? In order for me to recognize myself, I must have known myself prior to the act of recognition. Even if I am to recognize myself through the accidental attributes of the self, that is, the body and so forth, I must know that it is this self that matches this body, and this knowledge has to be present to the self at all times.

Aminrazavi (2003, 208) elaborates by claiming that the knowledge of myself, therefore, "has to be of a primary nature, an a priori concept that knows itself through itself directly and without mediation, and it is in this sense of knowing that 'consciousness through consciousness'".

Implications for Democratic Education

In appreciation of Ibn Sina's notion of intuition, any human action has the potential to be rational, imaginative and discerning. Human beings, therefore, are capable of rational and imaginative conceptualisation and practice.

By implication, when humans engage in democratic educational practices, their deliberations should be informed by cognitive and emotive activities of mind and heart, in terms of which such actions produce knowledge and understanding. And, when a person remains conscious of the existence of his or her self, he or she looks at his or her own pronouncements prior to considering others' views within democratic engagements.

The Ibn Sinian point of deliberation is that an individual will make more sense of others' views if he or she has clarity of his or her own views. Only then can his or her views be brought into conversation with what others have to say, and the possibility that his or her views might change happens as a result only after considering his or her views in discerning fashion in relation to others' views. Thus, the idea of an intuition of the self—as proposed by Ibn Sina—provokes an individual to make sense of what is known to him or her before considering such views in deliberation with others. As an intuitive being, humans are able to reflect upon themselves and others; they are able to imagine ways of being from different perspectives and hence to come to renewed realisations. And, when others' views in deliberative encounters are considered, the task of imagination, following Ibn Sina, would be to think of alternative possibilities that might not be immediately known to one—that is, to consider how things would be if more radical and unconforming ways of doing would be conceived. Here, we specifically refer to Ibn Sina's notion of *ma'rifah* (intuitive cognition) through which an individual immerses his or her thoughts in contemplation with the possibility to see things not thought of before—that is a "consciousness through consciousness" (Aminrazavi 2003, 208).

Following Ibn Sina, because human beings are not born with a predetermined set of knowledge, but rather as a blank tablet, they have the capacity to come to know and experience the world unaffected by any a priori knowledge. For this reason, human beings come to engage with and to know this through experiencing the other. Moreover, they come to know the world through experience—thereby actualising their potentiality through education. Such an understanding of how human beings come to know themselves, others and the world in which they find themselves brings particular enhancements to notions of democratic education. On the one hand, it suggests that human beings are not pre-designed in a certain way that might incline them towards certain viewpoints or perceptions of others and the world. Rather, they have the acquired capacity to embark upon their own paths of familiarity through their own experiences. On the other hand, as intuitive beings, their encounters and experiences are not constrained by only rational forms of engagement and deliberation. Instead, by virtue of their intuition, they are able to engage imaginatively, thereby opening themselves to the unexpected.

SUMMARY

In this chapter, we elucidated Ibn Sina's notion of intuition (*ḥads*) in relation to practices that are rational, imaginative and perceptive. We paid particular attention to his conceptions of knowledge and intuition (*ḥads*)— highlighting that to Ibn Sina, human beings do not only come into this world without any innate knowledge; they indeed have the potentiality to come to their own ways of seeing themselves, others and the world around them through their own experiences. By implication, human intuitive intelligence comprises both rational and emotive aspects. And, when humans engage in democratic educational practices, their deliberations should be underscored by both cognitive and emotive dimensions of knowing, acting and being.

REFERENCES

Aminrazavi, M. 2003. How Ibn Sīnian is Suhrawardī's Theory of Knowledge? *Philosophy East and West* 53 (2): 203–214.
Arif, S. 2000. Intuition and Its Role in Ibn Sina's Epistemology. *Al-Shajarah—Journal of the International Institute of Islamic Thought and Civilization* 5 (1): 95–126.
Aristotle. 1931. *De Anima*. Trans. J.A. Smith. Oxford: Clarendon University Press.
Duschinsky, R. 2012. Tabula Rasa and Human Nature. *Philosophy* 87: 509–529.
Eran, A. 2007. Intuition and Inspiration: The Causes of Jewish Thinkers' Objection to Avicenna's Intellectual Prophecy (Ḥads). *Jewish Studies Quarterly* 14 (1): 39–71.
Ibn Sina, A.A.H. 1975. *Al-Shifa al-Tabi-iyyat al-Nafs*. Ed. C. Anawati and S. Zayed. Cairo: Dar al-Kitab al-'Arabi.
Kabadayi, T. 2006. Aristotle and Avicenna Ibn Sina in Terms of the Theory of Intellects. *Uludağ University Faculty of Arts and Sciences Journal of Social Sciences* 7 (10): 15–27.
Locke, J. 1997. *An Essay Concerning Human Understanding*. London: Penguin Books.
Marmura, M.E. 1991. Plotting the Course of Avicenna's Thought. A Review: Avicenna and the Aristotelian Tradition: Introduction to Reading Avicenna's Philosophical Texts by Dimitri Gutas. *Journal of the American Oriental Society* 111 (2): 333–342.

Nazari, M. 2015. Avicenna (Ibn Sina) and Tabula Rasa. http://www.moradnazari.com/avicenna-ibn-sina-and-tabula-rasa/. Accessed 11 Apr 2019.
Nuseibeh, S. 2002. Epistemology. In *Encyclopaedia of Islamic Philosophy: Part II*, ed. S.H. Nasr, 824–840. Lahore: Suhail Academy.
Rahman, F. 1963. Ibn Sina. In *A History of Muslim Philosophy*, ed. M.M. Sharif, vol. 1, 480–505. Wiesbaden: Otto Harrassowitz.

CHAPTER 9

Fazlur Rahman's Notion of *Shura* and Its Implications for Democratic Education

Abstract In this chapter, we examine the centrality of *shura* as a deliberative practice in relation to the political, social, economic and private. As such, we show that *shura* is as necessary in matters of political governance as it is between spouses in relation to the rearing of their children. Thereafter, we examine some of the implications of Rahman's elucidation of *shura* for democratic education. Democratic education should remain open-ended and inconclusive as there is always more to know and to be deliberated on. That is, democratic education relies on forms of human engagement where the possibility is expanded for participants engaged in such practices to remain in potentiality. Likewise, Rahman's cooperative view of *shura* accentuates the need to include all people engaged about matters of public concern—most notably, those voices, who might be in disagreement, and who would be most likely to be excluded from any consultation and participation.

Keywords *Shura* (deliberative action) • Political governance • Potentiality • Consultation • Participation

INTRODUCTION

As a consequence of his discontent with the political landscape in his home country, Pakistan, and the opposition he received from Muslim conservative voices, Fazlur Rahman migrated to the United States and eventually settled in Chicago where he became known as a rational and highly influential Muslim scholar who studied the classics of Muslim theology. In this regard, Fazlur Rahman's (1982) contribution to the metaphysics of Islamic thought has some links with Ibn Sinian epistemology. However, it was his vehement intellectual onslaught against popular Sufism—especially being highly critical of established Muslim institutions like Al-Azhar University in Cairo—which gained much attention as he endeavoured to restore the rational impetus of Muslim educational discourse. Our interest in this chapter is in Rahman's (1982) exposition of the Qur'anic concept of *shura* and its implications for democratic education.

ON *SHURA* (DELIBERATIVE ENGAGEMENT) AND *UMMAH* (COMMUNITY)

As a historical and theological text, which invites its readers to engage critically with and to ponder on the words of God, the Qur'an is replete with verses and invocations, calling for *shura*—that is, mutual consultation or deliberative engagement. *Shura* is conceived as a broad principle of governance, engagement, elicitation of advice or counsel, deliberation and decision-making and cuts across various domains: the political, the economic, the social and the private. Furthermore, *shura* is primarily geared at engaging with the opinions of and arguments with others, so that different voices are taken into account; hence, preventing the possibility of autocratic decision-making and action. The Qur'an affirms that individuals—and hence communities—are capable of exercising independent thoughts and judgements. Individuals (and communities) are, therefore, able to deliberate on particular matters, and to arrive at particular conclusions.

As autonomous beings, humans have the capacity for independent judgement and for engaging in *shura*—that is, for engaging deliberatively with others. If one therefore considers, from an Islamic perspective, that the Qur'an conceives of *shura* (deliberative engagement), as an injunction through which humans ought to engage with others and with difference—that is, *wa amruhum shura bainahum* (those whose affairs are decided through mutual consultation)—then practices of any kind of exclusion and marginalisation can never be feasible forms of action. Stated differently, the foregrounding of *shura* (deliberative engagement) is premised on an understanding that human engagement is not predetermined or pre-conditioned on notions of sameness and agreement. Rather, the point of *shura* (deliberative engagement) is that human beings are under obligation to engage with difference and diverse perspectives, even when such perspectives are considered irreconcilable with their own.

Rahman (1984, 9) uses the Qur'anic dictum, *wa amruhum shura bainahum*, that is, human beings' common affairs are to be decided by their common and mutual consultation and discussion, as the basis of his argument. Firstly, *shura* (engagement) is not just reliant on the views and perspectives of a single individual, but rather an engagement that takes into consideration what is common to a community (*ummah*). The point is, a community is charged with contemplating and resolving communal matters. And, following Rahman (1984, 9), if a community is incapable of settling common affairs due to conditions of ignorance and hopelessness, then an *ummah* (community) should first be reconstructed and reconstituted (Rahman 1984, 9) before *shura* can be considered a way of resolving common affairs. In other words, *shura* is dependent on a community, based on particular principles of respect, regard and a willingness to engage with others and the views of others. Rahman (1984, 7) strongly objects to the prevalence of *shura* in the absence of a discerning *ummah*. In other words, if an *ummah* is not conscientious and committed to resolving common affairs, there is no point about *shura* at all. For him, "being ignorant and unenlightened" works against the democratic engagement of people, as such people cannot "discern right from wrong and legislate correctly" (Rahman 1984, 7).

Secondly, *shura* (engagement) is conditional on the "active goodwill and cooperation" of people (Rahman 1984, 4). If people do not show a willingness to want to engage, and if they do not show a readiness towards joint action, democratic engagement would not manifest. The point about democratic engagement is premised on the Qur'anic expression in Chap. 5 verse 2: *Wa ta'awanu ala al-birri wa al-taqwa wa la ta'awanu ala al-ithmi wa al-'udwan* (and cooperate in righteousness and piety, but do not cooperate in wrongdoing and transgression). Showing goodwill implies that people in engagement treat one another with civility. Being unduly disrespectful invariably leads to the exclusion of others from the engagement, and the possibility that the engagement will last is highly improbable.

For obvious reasons, cooperation is a necessary condition for engagement to occur but this does not imply that agreement should also be the result of cooperation. Rather, cooperation is imperative when people engage with openness to one another's diverse perspectives. Failing to remain open to others' points of view would result in anarchy and the disintegration of law and order (Rahman 1984, 6). And, when anarchy prevails, cooperation would be distanced from the engagement. As Kamali (2015, 63) notes, whenever consultation leads to consensus, "it becomes an important indicator by which to verify balanced and moderate positions in determination of issues". *Shura*, posits Kamali (2015, 112), is critical to participatory governance and realisation of well-moderated responses to issues of public concern. He maintains, "[i]t is through the understanding and recognition of different and sometimes opposing views to those of one's own, and one's openness toward reconciling divergent interests and concerns, that well-balanced solutions to issues can be expected to emerge" (Kamali 2015, 112).

Thirdly, Rahman (1984, 5) posits that *shura* involves "mutual discussions on an absolutely equal footing". Equality, as the basis for deliberative engagement, implies that no one should be excluded from the deliberation and, everyone on an egalitarian basis has the right to articulate his or her truth claims. No one can be internally excluded from deliberations just because his or her views do not gain the support of the majority of members of the group. The pronouncement of ill-conceived views cannot be taken as a reason to exclude members engaged democratically in deliberation. The idea of excluding people prematurely from deliberative engagements implies that such people do not have an opportunity to rescind their perhaps not carefully considered views. Excluding others with unpersuasive claims can also deny them opportunities to think differently about matters after they have encountered more convincing arguments. In this sense, equality implies that people must be respected for their views irrespective of whether such ways require more rigorous discernment. In line with the point made earlier, if members of an *ummah* (community) do not show an openness to listen to what others have to say—even if their (others') views are implausible—then the possibility that a community might become enlightened would be denied. This is different from refusing to become enlightened as would be associated with people who show a reluctance to become informed. Remaining unenlightened is a choice some people make and such a community—that is, one comprising of unenlightened persons—would not enhance any possibility of *shura* (deliberative engagement). Put differently, if some people refuse to be open and become enlightened, the practice of *shura* would not be justified.

Implications of *Shura* for Knowledge Construction

If one considers that *shura* is constitutive of human discernment, goodwill and cooperation as well as egalitarian action, then it follows that knowledge constructions among different people engaged democratically cannot be about attaining conclusiveness. This is so on the grounds that the possibility of dissensus would be rife considering that deliberative action is open to the pronouncement of a plurality of views and interpretations. Rahman (1982, 145) considers knowledge construction as open-ended on the basis of the following claim: "[i]t is obviously not necessary that a certain interpretation once accepted must continue to be accepted; there is always both room and necessity for new interpretations, and this is, in truth and ongoing process."

Based on the aforementioned understanding of the inconclusiveness of knowledge and interpretation, the claim that "knowledge is not open to revision ... but only to further elaboration and application" (Wan Daud 1997, 15) seems to be untenable because interpretation in itself is a particular perspective subjected to particular situational contexts, and when the contexts change, interpretations and reinterpretations might ensue. In this way, an interpretation of knowledge does not seem to be final, as varying contexts would render different and new interpretations—that is, revisions ensue that might be subjected to extensions and elaborations of meaning. Of course, the argument is used that the Qur'an and prophetic sayings are immutable. However, it is their interpretations that are changeable on the basis that such judgements are made by humans. Both established meanings of the Qur'an (*mukhkamat*) and ambiguous meanings (*mutashabihat*) constitute the Divine Revelation of God; yet, their interpretations according to the Qur'an itself might be subjected to rethinking by humans and, thus, open for possible reinterpretation and revision. Hence, we tend to agree with Rahman on his understanding of interpretation of the divine messages. For us, the Qur'an is a book of guidance without doubt (*shakk*); however, there can be conjecture (*zann*) about its interpretations as the human mind is fallible. In this regard, we concur with Rahman (1982, 145) that an interpretation of knowledge does not have to be connected to certainty (*yaqin*). On this basis, the necessity for *shura* is salient on the grounds that interpretations and reinterpretations can be put to critical scrutiny by people in deliberative fashion. If not, what would be the point of *shura*?

One of the implications of *shura* for democratic education is that *shura* affirms and foregrounds the rights of individuals to be consulted—that is, that decisions cannot be made without taking into account various opinions or viewpoints. The significance of *shura*, however, is its placing in relation to disagreement and dissensus. It goes without much explanation that practices of *shura* would be fairly straightforward in contexts and engagements of agreement and compliance. This, of course, would be less the case under conditions of debate or contestation. In *shura*, one finds a pre-conditioned practice of engaging and listening to the other—that is, engaging with mutual agreement to consult. It therefore becomes apparent that *shura* recognises that individuals, communities and societies do not always co-exist in mutual understandings and practices of assent. Rather, human beings, because of their capacity as autonomous thoughts and actions, are open to diverse and divergent perspectives. This in itself is a confirmation of the inherent pluralism, which embodies what it means to be in this world. With an acknowledgement of pluralism comes the recognition of difference. *Shura* proposes one way of navigating these differences.

Moreover, and finally, *shura* is contingent on the extent to which individuals and communities are open to others and their views and their willingness to engage with the perspectives of others. In this sense, engaging in *shura* has the potential, on the one hand, to bring into question undisputed or uninterrogated notions of being and thinking, such as, believing, for example, that teaching and learning are uni-directional processes, which unfold in a linear fashion and which are not open to deliberation and debate, or that the teacher is the only source of knowledge in a classroom. On the other hand, it is possible through *shura*, to embark on different pathways, which might not previously have been considered.

To us, the idea of *shura* holds significant potential and implications for teachers and their teaching of democratic education. Teachers, as we know, come into their classroom settings with set ideas of how they see they teaching and learning—that is, what ought to be taught and what ought to be learnt. Similarly, they have set ideas about who they are as 'the teacher', and who learners are in relation to the authority of 'the teacher'. We have particular concerns about the pre-establishment of such constructions of teaching, as we argue that such rigidity would be counter-intuitive to practices and pedagogies of democratic engagement. Underscoring this tension and our argument is that who teachers are is not only taken for granted but is submerged in normative practices and methodologies. *Shura* potentially brings within classroom settings reflection on both sets of identities—that is, the teacher and his or her students, so that all pre-existent certainties are brought into debate and consultation.

The point being made is that when teachers assume that all learners are the same, and that all learning unfolds in the same way, learning, in fact, seldom occurs. It is only when teachers begin to engage and deliberate with those they teach—with who they are and what they bring—that teaching can find its connection with learning, and when the teacher finds a connection with his or her students. This requires an openness on the part of the teacher. It requires a willingness by the teacher to think critically about who he or she is and how he or she might be experienced by those he or she teaches. Moreover, it requires of the teacher a willingness to reconsider particular practices and habits, so that the pedagogical encounter is expanded rather than constrained.

Summary

We commenced this chapter by drawing on the Qur'an to demonstrate the centrality of *shura* as a deliberative practice in relation to political, social, economic and private spheres. We showed that *shura* is as necessary in matters of political governance as it is between spouses in relation to the rearing of their children. The question remains: what are some of the implications of Rahman's elucidation of *shura* for democratic education? Democratic education should remain open-ended and inconclusive as there is always more to know and on which to deliberate. In other words, democratic education relies on forms of human engagement where the possibility is expanded for participants engaged in such practices to remain in potentiality.

Likewise, Rahman's cooperative view of *shura* accentuates the need to include all people engaged in matters of public concern—most notably, those voices that might be in disagreement and who would most likely be excluded from any consultation and participation. It is certainly not uncommon for particular individuals or groups of people to be silenced because of their viewpoints. Likewise, the potential contributions and viewpoints of people who might be considered unimportant or 'less-than' might be reduced or dismissed, on the basis that what they have to say holds no value. Here, we immediately think of the millions of refugees and immigrants, who experience untold hardship and marginalisation in their desperate search for civility and peaceful existence and coexistence—especially in the contexts of liberal democracies. Whatever they might have to say about themselves and their plight has no bearing on the often harsh decisions, which decide their fate. If people are excluded on the grounds of not having something worthwhile to say, the possibility that they actually might be heard and their views taken into consideration would be denied which, in turn, would render democratic education an impossibility. Finally, a *shura* grounded in the possibility of (re)interpretation dismisses the notion that understandings in and about democratic education would be absolute and that there is nothing more to come to know.

References

Kamali, M.H. 2015. *The Middle Path of Moderation in Islam: The Qur'anic Principle of Wasatiyyah*. Oxford: Oxford University Press.

Rahman, F. 1982. *Islam and Modernity*. Chicago, IL: The University of Chicago Press.

———. 1984. The Principle of *Shura* and the Role of the *Umma* in Islam. *American Journal of Islamic Studies* 1 (1): 1–9.

Wan Daud, W.M.N. 1997. Islamization of Contemporary Knowledge: A Brief Comparison Between Al-Attas and Fazlur Rahman. *Al-Shajarah—Journal of the International Institute of Islamic Thought and Civilization* 2 (1): 1–19.

CHAPTER 10

Muhammad Iqbal's Conception of *Ijtihad* and Its Implications for Democratic Education

Abstract In this chapter, we analyse Iqbal's understanding of the practice of *ijtihad* that is inherently spiritual. In other words, implicit in his understanding and practice is the notion that people are not just open and reflective about the human relations in becoming—that is, relations of cooperation, coexistence and recognition of one another. Also, what Iqbal's exposition of the practice of *ijtihad* encourages are forms of living whereby people become deeply (i.e., spiritually) concerned about their own, perhaps unwarranted practices. Introspection and a commitment towards identifying their deficiencies would become enabling practices to enhance human co-belonging and recognition of one another for the reason that people are prepared to take into critical scrutiny what they hold to be true. Their spiritual recognition that their own practices might be deeply flawed and in need of reparations is a profound recognition of *ijtihadi* proportions. That is, when people have internalised the fallibility of their own practices would they become more open to new re-beginnings. In this way, democratic education becomes a practice of immense spiritual propensity in the sense that people would be prepared and willing to amend distortions associated with their own indigenous ways of being and acting.

Keywords *Ijtihad* (intellectual exertion) • Human co-belonging • Spirituality • Fallibility

Introduction

At a time when the Muslim and Western worlds have been overtaken by fear and disillusionment, it was Muhammad Iqbal who emerged as a beacon of hope to re-establish much-needed political deliberations between the two worlds (Malik 2013, 8). According to Fateh Mohammad Malik (2013, 8), reverting to Muhammad Iqbal's political thought could "reopen the lines of communication *within* the Muslim world and *between* the Muslim and Western worlds". Our attraction to Iqbal's thoughts is based on an understanding that there is no dichotomy between religion and politics in Islam and that any attempt at separating the two would be anathema to the spirit of Islam. As purported by Iqbal (1988, cited in Malik 2013, 11, 13), in "Islam God and the universe, spirit and matter, Church and State, are organic to each other ... [and] creating a false disconnect between religion and politics would rob a dynamic faith of its practical possibilities". In this regard, Iqbal's notion of religion is inclusive and the "purpose of Islam is to create a society that holds all people, irrespective of their religion and nations, in high esteem and respect" (Malik 2013, 13).

Muhammad Iqbal, on whom scholars like Fazlur Rahman drew for liberatory thoughts in and about Islam, championed the notion of reason and experience as enunciated in the Qur'an. For Iqbal, Islam has a democratic spirit, evident from its insistence that *shura* (mutual consultation) and *ijma* (consensus of a community) should be revisited in Islamic discourse (Iqbal 1988). *Ijtihad* (intellectual exertion) and *shura* (mutual consultation) are interdependent processes; *ijtihad* (intellectual exertion) should always be used in the quest to derive at tenable collective and critical judgements on the premise of *shura* (mutual consultation) (Davids and Waghid 2016). In this chapter, we examine one particular practice, namely *ijtihad* (exertion), in relation to Iqbal's assertion that Islam has a democratic ethos. Thereafter we look at some of the implications of *ijtihad* for democratic education.

Ijtihad in Iqbal's Political Thought

According to Kamali (2002, 617):

> [*Jihad* and *ijtihad*] are both are derived from the same root j-h-d, which signifies striving, whether physical or intellectual, on the part of a Muslim or

a group of Muslims to advance a cause they believe to be of merit and that would hopefully earn them the pleasure of God.

Shabbar (2018, 1) clarifies that the trilateral root j-h-d, vocalised either as *jahada* or *jahuda*, denotes the action of expending effort. According to Shabbar (2018, 1), most lexicons, among them Lisān al-'Arab, "distinguish between jahada and jahuda, with jahada referring simply to the expenditure of effort, and jahuda denoting the same process, but with an added element of hardship and difficulty". Although the term *ijtihad* itself does not occur anywhere in the Qur'an, the sense conveyed by this word is found in numerous places throughout the Qur'an (Shabbar 2018). According to Kamali (2005, 315):

> Ijtihad is the most important source of Islamic law next to the Qur'an and the Sunnah. The main difference between ijtihad and the revealed sources of the Shari'ah lies in the fact that ijtihad is a continuous process of development whereas divine revelation and prophetic legislation discontinued upon the demise of the Prophet. In this sense, ijtihad continues to be the main instrument of interpreting the divine message and relating it to the changing conditions of the Muslim community in its aspirations to attain justice, salvation and truth.

To Kamali (2002, 623)

> [*Ijtihad*] literally means striving or self-exertion; it may be defined as a creative but disciplined and comprehensive intellectual effort to derive juridical rulings on given issues from the sources of the Shari'ah in the context of the prevailing circumstances of the Muslim society [with an emphasis 'creative thinking', and 'the prevailing conditions of society'].

In this regard, Kamali (2002) provides the following elaboration on his understanding:

> Ijtihad is basically designed to address new and unprecedented issues and often seeks to provide a fresh interpretation of the source materials of the Shari'āh relating to the new issues. Creative intellectual exertion also means that existing ideas and teachings of others are not taken at face value nor imitated, but scrutinised and their relevance to new issues is independently ascertained. Ijtihad is the most important source of the Shari'āh next to the Qur'ān and Sunnah. The main difference between ijtihād and the revealed

sources of the Shari'āh lies in the fact that ijtihād is a continuous process of development whereas the revelation of the Qur'ān and the Prophetic legislation discontinued with the demise of the Prophet (peace be on him). Ijtihad as such continues to be the main instrument of relating the messages of the Qur'ān and the Sunnah to the changing conditions of the Muslim community in its quest for justice, salvation and truth.

Our own etymological analysis of the practice of *ijtihad* is premised on Edward W Lane's depiction of the term, namely exerting the faculties of the mind to the utmost (Lane 1984, 473). According to the Sunan Abu Dawud (1984, 687), *ijtihad* means to perform an intellectual judgement. Lane elucidates *ijtihad* (1984, 605) as an intellectual action "suitable to the requirements of wisdom, justice, right or rightness". The notion of *ijtihad* as exertion finds expression in the seminal thoughts of Iqbal (1988, 148–149) (our italics):

> The word literally means to *exert*. In the terminology of Islamic law it means to exert with a view to form an *independent judgment* on a legal question … [which] has its origin in a well-known verse of the Qur'an—'And to those who exert We show Our path' … [that is, it] embodies … an intellectual attitude.

What we understand from Iqbal (1988) is that the Qur'an, even as a divine text, cannot be understood and put into practice without some element of human interpretation. Human beings come to texts and other interactions with their own worldviews and frameworks through which they make sense and internalise what they encounter. Whatever knowledge they acquire, therefore, is processed through those frameworks and how they relate to that knowledge within their particular contexts. For this reason, Dallmayr (2011) argues that in the divine-human encounter not only human beings are transformed (their understanding deepened and enlarged), but that also the meaning of the divine is transformed into a personally experienced God (or divine presence). According to Dallmayr (2011)

> [This means] that the divine has been powerfully re-interpreted and re-thought. As a result, the interpreter is no longer a target of external (possibly clerical) control or manipulation, but he/she becomes a partner or participant in the transmission of the divine message—[d]ifferently put: religious faith is humanized and democratized.

In continuing, Iqbal's view of *ijtihad* (intellectual exertion) is articulated by him as freedom to rebuild Islamic law (*Shariah*) in the light of "modern thought and experience" (Iqbal 1984, 157). Put differently, for Iqbal, *ijtihad* is autonomous intellectual judgement, commensurate with 'modern Islam', that is, producing "fresh interpretation[s] of its principles" (Iqbal 1984, 163). This view resonates with that of Kamali (2002, 624), who asserts:

> [A]s a vehicle of renewal and reform, ijtihād was always dominated by its dual concern: on the one hand by the continuity of the given fundamentals of Islam, and on the other, by attempting to keep pace with the realities of social change.

Moreover, in its emphasis on exertion, and in its inclinations towards interpretation and reinterpretation, *ijtihad* embodies a particular flexibility and an openness to other considerations. In this sense, *ijtihad* infers a willingness to listen to and learn from others, and to be open to the possibility that what one has held as truth might, in fact, not be so. When dealing with texts of definitive meaning and reliability, which deal with subsidiary, mundane issues, Shabbar (2018, 5) contends, "[*ijtihad*] does not permanently abrogate a ruling that was derived from the text at an earlier time; however, it might go beyond the previous ruling".

What is quite poignant about Iqbal's understanding of *ijtihad* is the connection he makes between intellectual exertion and the cultivation of humanity. In his words

> Humanity needs three things today—a spiritual interpretation of the universe, spiritual emancipation of the individual, and basic principles of a universal import directing the evolution of human society on a spiritual basis. (Iqbal 1984, 179)

What seems to emanate from Iqbal's understanding of *ijtihad* is that, firstly, interpretation and reinterpretation, such as through intellectual exertion, are not only independent human judgements, but also acts of spirituality. In this sense, Iqbal's idea of *ijtihad* resonates with an act of emotion. Secondly, *ijtihad* should enable the emancipation of individuals from that which seems to constrain their thinking. Thirdly, *ijtihad* should be linked to cultivating a society that invokes spirituality—that is, looking beyond merely acting rationally by also extending such actions towards transcendental realities. In line with such an understanding of *ijtihad*, we next examine its implications for democratic education.

DEMOCRATIC EDUCATION AND *IJTIHAD*

As discussed in this chapter, the emancipatory potential of *ijtihad* resides in an understanding that diverse viewpoints can be brought into public deliberation whereby people's thinking and acting can be liberated—if need be—from what they previously endeared. To become emancipated is tantamount to be freed from those ways of seeing events in the world that constrain human interaction and good living (Davids and Waghid 2016). As explained by Davids and Waghid (2016, 65), the Qur'an differentiates between knowledge (which is *muhkamāt*, that is foundational or decisive), and knowledge (which is *mutashābihāt*, that is allegorical or unspecific). According to al-Qaradawi (date, cited in Shabbar 2018, 5), *ijtihad* holds the following conditions:

- every effort is made to arrive at complete clarity on the issue at hand;
- definitive issues are not subject to *ijtihad*;
- speculative texts and rulings must not be treated as though they were definitive;
- work should be done to bridge the chasm that presently exists between the juristic and tradition-based schools of thought;
- beneficial new insights should be welcomed; and
- there is a need for a shift to communal *ijtihad*, since the view of an entire group is more likely to be correct than that of a single individual.

As espoused by al-Qaradawi (date, cited in Safian 2016, 52), rigid interpretation must be avoided—for instance, in addressing the pressing needs of Muslim communities living in the West. Their needs and problems, argues al-Qaradawi, are unique; therefore, attention should be given to devising exceptional rulings pertaining to their unique circumstances (al-Qaradawi date, cited in Safian 2016, 52). As we turn our attention to *ijtihad* and democratic education, we are especially interested in *ijtihad* in relation to communal benefit and advancement, as might be realised through *ijma* (consensus of a community). To Kamali (1997, 215), the essence of *ijma* lies in the natural growth of ideas.

[It begins, he says] with the personal *ijtihād* of individual jurists and culminates in universal acceptance of a particular opinion over a period of time. Differences of opinion are tolerated until a consensus emerges and in the process, there is no room for compulsion or imposition of ideas upon the community.

Of course, we would agree that, while consensus is a desirable outcome of engagement, it should not necessarily be an enabling condition for engagement. Instead, we would argue that both individual autonomy and *ijtihad* should be aimed at enabling *ijma*. In this way, the possibility exists that the ideas or interpretations of an individual or a community can be interrupted or re-directed on the grounds that more credible understandings ensue. Since *ijma* reflects the natural evolution and acceptance of ideas in the life of the community, the basic notion of *ijma* can never be expected to discontinue, explains Kamali (2005, 157). Kamali (2005, 158) continues

[T]he question as to whether the law, as contained in the divine sources, has been properly interpreted is always open to a measure of uncertainty and doubt, especially in regard to the deduction of new rules by way of analogy and ijtihad.

Kamali (2005, 158) states that, where communities or scholars differ in relation to interpretations and understandings, *ijma* serves as "an instrument of tolerance", and as such, provides Islam with a potential for freedom of movement and a capacity for evolution.

Following on the above is a recognition that human interactions and engagements with texts, ideas or other human beings are always open to diverse interpretations and disagreement. Different worldviews, therefore, are considered a natural and necessary part of societal and social engagement. For this reason, the necessity of *ijtihad*, as well as *shura* and *ijma*, becomes evident—if humans are to find a way of meaningful and peaceful engagement and peaceful coexistence.

In concluding, Iqbal's (1984) assertion that *ijtihad* (intellectual exertion) has an inherently democratic and spiritual ethos stems from his concern to resolve challenging matters regarding human cooperation and coexistence. And, considering that he was mainly concerned with the disdain the Muslim community at the time showed towards experiential reasoning in and about their malaise, he became adamant that the Qur'an and Hadith (prophetic sayings), the foundational sources of Islam, should be subjected to more independent analyses—that is, interpretations and reinterpretations—imbued with possibilities to see others' points of view (democratic inclinations) and treating them (others) with a deep sense of respect for the human spirit in relation to its vexed contexts. Put differently, Iqbal's (1984) claims about *ijtihad* lie in the possibilities of the practice offering democratic human action.

Iqbal's (1984) defence of *ijtihad* is premised on the notion that humans can learn to live with one another's diverse perspectives and that difference does not have to become a licence to discriminate against one another. To embark on emancipatory practices is conditional upon a practice of *ijtihad* that can attune one another to just human actions. A community that thrives on practising *ijtihad* would be able to act in one another's interest without misrecognising the views of others that might be different from their own. The point is, an emancipatory *ijtihad* summons humans to engage with diversity and difference to the extent where the other is recognised for his or her otherness without prejudice and intolerance towards that which is different and other. Only then, would humans be emancipated and would their free use of *ijtihad* inspire them to act with civility and love for one another.

Summary

As a fitting tribute in recognition of Iqbal's monumental contribution to a rational-cum-emotive understanding of Muslim education, a tombstone has been erected in his honour in the Mevlana Rumi Museum in Konya, Turkey. He advocated a practice of *ijtihad* that is inherently spiritual. In other words, implicit in his understanding and practice is the notion that people are not just open and reflective about the human relations in becoming, that is, relations of cooperation, coexistence and recognition of one another. Iqbal's exposition of the practice of *ijtihad* encourages forms of living whereby people become deeply (i.e., spiritually) concerned about their own, perhaps unwarranted, practices. Introspection and a commitment towards identifying their deficiencies would become enabling practices to enhance human co-belonging and recognition of one another for the reason that people are prepared to take into critical scrutiny what they hold to be true. Their spiritual recognition that their own practices might be deeply flawed and in need of reparation is a profound recognition of *ijtihadi* proportions. That is, when people have internalised the fallibility of their own practices they would become more open to new re-beginnings. In this way, democratic education becomes a practice of immense spiritual propensity in the sense that people would be prepared and willing to amend distortions associated with their own indigenous ways of being and acting.

REFERENCES

Dallmayr, F. 2011. Opening the Doors of Ijtihad. Reset Dialogues on Civilizations. https://www.resetdoc.org/story/opening-the-doors-of-ijtihad/. Accessed 17 Apr 2019.

Davids, N., and Y. Waghid. 2016. *Ethical Dimensions of Muslim Education*. New York: Palgrave Macmillan.

Iqbal, M. 1984. *The Reconstruction of Religious Thought in Islam*. Lahore: Iqbal Academy.

———. 1988. *The Reconstruction of Religious Thought in Islam*. Lahore: Muhammad Ashraf.

Kamali, H. 1997. *Freedom of Expression in Islam*. Cambridge: Islamic Texts Society.

Kamali, M.H. 2002. Issues in the Understanding of Jihād and Ijtihād. *Islamic Studies* 41 (4): 617–634.

———. 2005. *Principles of Islamic Jurisprudence*. Cambridge: Islamic Texts Society.

Lane, E.W. 1984. *Arabic-English Lexicon*. Vol. 1 and 2. Cambridge: Islamic Text Society Trust.

Malik, F.M. 2013. *Reconstruction of Muslim Political Thought*. Islamabad: National Book Foundation.

Safian, Y. 2016. The Contribution of Yusuf Qaradawi to the Development of Fiqh. *Electronic Journal of Islamic and Middle Eastern Law* 4: 45–53. http://www.ejimel.uzh.ch/. Accessed 18 Apr 2019.

Shabbar, S. 2018. *Ijtihad and Renewal*. Trans. N. Roberts. Herndon: International Institute of Islamic Thought.

Sunan Abu Dawud, 1984. Hadith. https://www.kalamullah.com/sunan-abu-dawood.html. Accessed 4 Aug 2019.

Coda: Democratic Education as an Act of *Ibadah*

Introduction

We have not encountered writings in Muslim traditions that eulogise democratic education as an act in service of God—that is, an act of *ibadah*. In Muslim traditions, *ibadah* is predominantly associated with the performance of rituals such as prayer (*salah*), fasting (*siyam*) and invocation (*du'a*). In the Muslim tradition of Imam Shafi'i—one of the prominent Sunni jurists in Islam—in which we were reared, education is also considered an *ibadah* in the sense that service in attendance of Allah cannot be disassociated from a form of human engagement, namely education. To seek education, to be educated and, indeed, to propagate education are all considered acts of *ibadah*. And, the argument that human engagement is associated with education implies that *ibadah* (service to God) should be extended to cultivating humanity. In this coda, we offer some thoughts on how the cultivation of humanity can be linked to enactments of *ibadah*, such as deliberative engagement and acting in association with one another with the intent of acting with justice.

Ibadah as an Act of Deliberative Engagement

Our focus on expositing *ibadah* is premised on an understanding that acting in the service of God is concomitantly connected with serving humanity. The point is that serving humanity is a godly act, in other words, an act of spirituality that invokes the human emotions. *Ibadah* can be associated with three human actions: firstly, to act with *ibadah* one renders oneself in service to God and humanity. This implies that one acknowledges humans on account of who they are and not what one expects of them. In this way, one acts respectfully towards other humans in honour of God's creation. Secondly, honouring humans means that one acknowledges them and pursues relationships with them. One does not act alone and with others, one engages through listening, articulation and talking back—that is, engaging in public deliberation with others. One's acts of *ibadah* are constrained by one's commitment to engage with others, without which one cannot claim to be in service of God. Thirdly, *ibadah* is an act of searching collectively for a common humanity. This does not mean that all humans should be the same, but rather that through their similarities and differences, humans endeavour to cultivate a common humanity in terms of which they strive to treat one another with dignity and respect. Hence, the practice of *ibadah* is associated with collective human engagement without which the cultivation of a common humanity would not be possible. However, when humans are performing *ibadat* (plural of *ibadah*) they endeavour to recognise one another and engage themselves in deliberation on the basis of respect and one another's contending views. Put differently, to perform *ibadah* is a highly rational and emotive act of human engagement for serving God and is inextricably connected to cultivating humanity in other words, acting democratically.

Ibadah as an Act of Justice

The Qur'an is replete with exhortations inviting human beings to act with justice as synonymous with performing *ibadat*. In *Surah al-Baqarah* (Chap. 2, verse 186 of the Qur'an) the following is stated:

> *Wa itha sa alaka 'ibadi 'anni fa inni qarib ujibu da'watadda'i itha da'an fal yastajibuli wal yu' minu bi la'allahum yarshudun* (And when my servants ask you [O Muhammad], concerning Me—indeed I am near. I respond to the invocation of the supplicant when he calls upon Me [by obedience] and believe in Me that they may be [rightly] guided).

In the above verse, the *yarshudun* (rightly guided people) can be associated with those who submit themselves in obedience to God and, by implication, are responsive to humanity. In this way, they (the rightly guided people) can be associated with those who pursue just action. Therefore, it is not unusual to connect the notion of *ibadah* (in service to God) to the practice of acting justly in relation to humanity. To be near to God (in *ibadah*) as the verse accentuates can also be associated with the following just actions towards humanity: firstly, being in proximity to God is a manifestation that humans embark on actions of a godly nature—that is, their activities are imbibed with actions such as treating other humans with civility. And, when they do so, they also recognise that they need to cultivate ethical relationships among themselves and others. Secondly, considering that God (Allah) is associated with compassion (*rahman*) and forgiveness (*rahim*), they endeavour to cultivate human relationships from which compassionate and forgiving human actions ensue. Simply put, their *ibadat* (in service to God) are most pertinently geared towards compassionate, humane and tolerant actions. Thirdly, being in service to God (*ibadat*) is inextricably intertwined with enactments of just and righteous actions. As aptly reminded in the Qur'an (16: 90):

> *Inna Allah ha ya'muru bil 'adl wal ihnsan wa ita ithil qurba wa yanha 'anil fahsha i wal munkari wal bagh yi ya'ithukum la 'alkum tathakkarun* (Indeed, Allah orders justice and good conduct and giving to relatives and forbids immorality and bad conduct and oppression. He admonishes you that perhaps you will be reminded) Qur'an.

Evident from the above verse of the Qur'an, just action (*'adl*) and good conduct (*ihsan*) are considered interrelated acts of *ibadat* (in service to God). Ultimately, the purposes of performing such acts of *ibadat* are geared towards resisting and restraining corruption, incivility and oppression. In this sense, *ibadah* (in service to God) becomes a highly politicised and liberatory act of justice. The problem in many communities is that *ibadah* (in service to God) is considered a narcissistic practice where individuals consider only their devotion to God as being in service of God. That is, they understand *ibadah* as a literal action of being in service to God, as in practices of worship and devotion, instead of recognising that service to God is also made manifest in service to humanity. Such a parochial view of *ibadah* compromises the more service-related conception of *ibadah*, which clearly repudiates injustice and incivility towards humanity.

One of the pillars of Islam and one of the highest *ibadah* (in service to God) is the performance of pilgrimage to Makkah (*hajj*), which is described as follows in the Qur'an (2: 197):

Hajj is [during] well-known months, so whoever has made *hajj* obligatory upon him- or herself therein [by entering the state of ihram], there is [to be for him or her] no sexual relations and no disobedience [*fusuq*] and no disputing during *hajj*. And whatever good you do—Allah knows it. And take provisions, but indeed, the best provision is fear of Allah. And fear Me, O you of understanding.

God admonishes humans to not indulge in *fusuq* (corruption), which invariably is detrimental to the pursuit of just action. Here, *fusuq* (corruption) is mentioned in contrast to the *ibadah* of *hajj* (pilgrimage), which suggests that the cultivation of humanity would be undermined by unscrupulousness and wrongdoing. Here, we specifically think of the horrific ways in which migrants are treated today. In many instances, they are denied access to many countries of their choice, they are discriminated against on the grounds of their religious beliefs and they are denied opportunities for employment despite having been accepted into their new countries of origin. To act democratically and educationally, for that matter, would be tantamount to treating humans with respect and dignity. The actions of several governments all over the world against the migration of people are indicative that *fusuq* (corruption and alienation) is rife and that democratic education is missing from the actions of such peoples.

The Qur'an is explicit in its exhortation "You are the best people ever raised for the good of mankind because you have been raised to serve others; you enjoin what is good and forbid evil and believe in Allah" (3: 111). In addition to emphasising the significance of being of service to God's creation, this verse confirms the social responsibility of humans—that is, of not only being cognisant of the strife and difficulties of others but also a preparedness to act for the sake of God. From this, it becomes clear that notions of being and doing good are not limited to an individual's relationship with God, but rather such notions indicate the extent to which individuals enact their responsibilities to God's creation, which in itself is a practice of worship. Similar exhortations are made with regard to extensions of gratitude and appreciation—not only in relation to God but also in relation to others, as a manifestation of gratitude to God. One reads, for example: "And [remember] when your Lord proclaimed, 'If you are grateful, I will surely increase you [in favour]'" (Qur'an 14: 7); "Any who is grateful does so to the profit of his own soul" (Qur'an 31: 12). When human beings show gratitude to others, this is a form of worship, since it reflects gratitude to God.

Pursuant to the above understanding of *ibadah* (service to God), it makes no sense when humans turn a blind eye to intolerance and corruption in communities. At the time of writing this coda, New Zealand had just suffered its worst terrorist attack during which 50 Muslim congregants were brutally gunned down in two mosques in Christchurch. That this act took place, while people were in prayer, in a house of worship is of course especially distressing, since it suggests a particular vulnerability and spirituality of the congregants, which was, no doubt, the primary motivation for the perpetrator's choice of venue and time (the attack took place during the Friday congregational prayers, referred to as *Jumuah*). It would subvert any person's *ibadah* (in service to God) not to speak out against such vile and intolerant acts of crime against fellow humans. And, it would be equally uncaring and improper not to respond justly to the suffering endured by the bereaved relatives and families of those so injudiciously murdered in places of *ibadat*. But then, of course, to be unjustly murdered in prayer (*salah*) only because someone else detests one's faith is reminiscent of the times of today: intolerance, hostility, even hatred, based on no other reason than choosing not to understand the identities and lifeworlds of others.

Yet, inasmuch as contemporary political rhetoric raises complex and disturbing questions about the type of world in which we find ourselves, and the inherent climate of intolerance, which seems to pervade particular pockets of societies and communities, we maintain that *ibadah* (service to God) offers a beacon of hope, that there are humans who stand firmly against injustice, intolerance and rebellion—in other words, those who champion the cause of democratic education. This has been evident not only in the response of New Zealand's Prime Minister Jacinda Ardern, but in the communal mobilisation and empathy. In these acts of empathy, it becomes evident that for most people, quite generally, living with intolerance and hostility towards others is simply not a way of life, and that differences among people should not be misconstrued as ignorance of the other.

At the heart of our motivation for writing a book that offers a dual perspective of what might otherwise be described as 'Western philosophy' and 'Muslim philosophy' was a desire to collapse these surface boundaries, which seemingly serve no other purpose but to categorise knowledge in terms of how people think they ought to see knowledge, which is in a rigid, enframed form. However, this is not the case. Knowledge lives and shifts through the engagements and lived realities of people; it spreads through reading and speech, during times of strife and peace. Knowledge is not barricaded into boxes, which is why, as shown in this book, 'Muslim philosophy' is as connected to Greek philosophy, as it is to 'Western' or communitarian philosophy. What distinguishes these philosophies is the author and his or her perspectives. What connects these philosophies, however, are those who read and live these philosophies.

Summary

In this coda (and the book in general), we have shown that different traditions of thought and practice can be brought into conversation with one another. Inasmuch as democratic education might at first not be seen as commensurate with a notion of *ibadah* (in service to God), we have shown that the possibility is there for concepts and practices from multiple traditions of thought and practice to be commensurate with democratic forms of being and acting. If such an analysis of ideas would enhance the rigorous tradition of analytic philosophy of education, then we would equally endeavour to make such analyses manifest in much of our ensuing works. Muhammad Iqbal and Fazlur Rahman, in particular, are shining examples of making assertive efforts to reconcile their seminal thoughts with those of their like-minded Western counterparts. Our work in and about democratic education began with revisiting salient concepts as espoused by leading Anglo-Saxon philosophers of education. Afterwards, we found it necessary to connect and enhance these philosophers' thoughts with those in Muslim-oriented environments. Our intellectual efforts throughout this book and as accentuated in the coda to the book are an attempt to elucidate multiple understandings of education and democratic action. It is, therefore, quite possible to assert that there is always potential for new becomings and new re-beginnings of thought to be introduced into discourses of democratic education.

Index[1]

A
Academic
  achievement, 22
  life, x
  performance, 42
  realm, 2
Account
  debt, 29
  recognition, 29
Action
  with compassion, 52
  democratic, 114
  emotive, 58
  with impunity, 45
  just, 111, 112
  Prophet Muhammad, 63
  rational, 19, 40
  self-determination, 3, 20
  in service of God, x, 109
Actions
  autonomous, 3, 4, 96
  compassionate, xv, 52–56, 58, 111

culpable, 53
deliberative, 78, 95
democratic, xv
emotive, xv, 28, 40, 50
human (*see* Human, actions)
just, 65, 111
principled, 31
righteous, 111
similar, 52
Adab, xv, 61–69
Agency, 21, 51
  human (*see* Human, agency)
Alienation, 22, 42, 69, 112
Appreciation
  demonstration of, 28
  expression of, 28
Argumentation
  critical, 57
  persuasive, 54
  rational, 19, 58
Autonomous
  freedom (*see* Freedom, autonomous)
  humans (*see* Humans, autonomous)

---

[1] Note: Page numbers followed by 'n' refer to notes.

B

Belligerence
  action, 40
  confrontation, 42, 43
  notions of, xiv
Benefactor, 28–30

C

Care, xiii, 29, 55, 84
  nuances of, xv
Citizenship
  affective, ix
  democratic, 29, 31, 40, 56, 57
  requirements of, 57
Classroom, 4, 6, 9, 52, 96
  settings, 96, 97
Co-dependence, 10–12
Co-learning, 2–12
Community, xiv, 15, 21, 29, 36, 37, 56, 64, 65, 92–94, 96, 105, 106, 111, 113
  consensus of, 100, 104
Compassion
  act with, 54, 57
  discussion of, 51
Confrontation
  ethical (*see* Ethical, confrontation)
  human (*see* Human, confrontation)
Controversy, 15, 16, 18, 20–22, 24, 25, 42, 69
Cooperation, 93–95, 105, 106
Criticism, 18, 39

D

Deliberation
  discourse of, 18
  moral, 41
  political, 97, 100
  public, 17, 55, 104, 110
Democracy
  constitutional, 16
  deliberative, 9, 10
  liberal, 18n1, 20, 21, 24, 69, 98
  questions of, 23
Democratic
  citizen, 29
  citizenship, 29, 31, 40, 56, 57
  dialogue, 21
  engagement, 11, 22, 77, 78, 87, 93, 96
  ethos, 100, 105
  institutions, 17
  justice, 6, 18, 19, 50, 56–58
  opinion formation, 18
  people, 19, 25
  reflexivity, 20
  will-formation, 17, 20
Dialogue, 8, 41–43
  respectful, 69
Dignity, 31, 110, 112
Disagreement, xiv, 6, 15, 21, 45, 46, 69, 96, 97, 105
Discourse, 18
  of deliberation, 7–11, 17, 19, 20, 24, 46, 47, 55, 64, 87, 88, 92, 94, 96, 100, 104, 110
  educational, 53, 92
  Islamic, 100
  pedagogical, xiv
  practical, 24, 25
  public, 23
Discrimination, 16, 44, 46, 56
  form of, 24
Dissensus, 10, 16, 21, 69, 95, 96
Dissent, 18, 19, 24, 44–47
Distress
  emotional, 44
  emotions of, 47
  moral (*see* Moral, distress)
Doctoral
  journey, 50, 53
  level, 52
  pedagogy (*see* Pedagogy, doctoral)
  research, 52

students, 51, 58
studies, 50, 53, 56, 58
supervision (*see* Supervision, doctoral)

E

Education
compassionate democratic, 50, 56–58
democratic, 40, 41, 43, 47, 50–58, 61–69, 71–78, 81–88, 91–98, 100–107, 109–114
democratic citizenship, 31, 40, 56, 57
discourse (*see* Discourse, educational)
general, ix, 66
higher (*see* Higher education)
initiatives, 32
philosophers of, 114
practices, 40, 50, 67, 74, 77, 87, 88
theory, xv, 52, 82
Educators, x, 7
Emotion
act of, x, 16, 36, 53, 103
claims of, xv
of freedom, xiv, 2
painful, 53
of talking back, 12, 15–25
Emotional
agitation, 41
dimension, 25, 67–69, 85, 88
distress, 39–47
labour, 52
trauma, 52
troubles, 33
turmoil, 42
well-being, 53
will formation, 25
Emotions
claims of, xv
nature of, ix
political, ix

role of, ix
significance of, xiii
will of, 19
Emotive, xv, xvi, 11, 12, 19, 25, 28–30, 40, 50, 51, 53, 54, 58, 85–88, 110
judgements, xv, 50, 51, 53, 54, 58
Empathy, xiii, 31, 52–55, 57, 113
acts of, 113
Encounter
cultural, 41
deliberative, x, 17, 87
democratic, 67, 69
democratic educational, 43
distressful, 41, 42, 44
educational, 43–46, 69
human, 16–19, 28, 41, 42, 67–69
teaching–learning, xiv
Encounters
deliberative, x, 17
pedagogical, 40, 97
Engagement
of agreement, 21, 96
co-dependent, 10, 11
convergences of, xiv
deliberative, 12, 78, 92–94, 109–110
democratic, 10, 22, 47, 77, 78, 87, 93–95
mutual, 47, 96
outcome of, 105
rational, 88, 110
Equality
of participation, 17, 18
sexual, 24
social, 23, 24
Ethical
code, 65
conciliation, 43
confrontation, 42, 45–47
dilemma, 45
practices, 64
regression, 42
relationships, 111

Ethics, 35, 62, 63
Exclusion
  mass, 21, 92
  practices of, 22
Experiences
  debilitating, 54
  educational, xv
  emotive, 19, 28
  instinctive, 76
  lived, 8, 54
  own, 52, 87, 88
  perceptual, 76

F
Fairness, 17, 47
Forgiveness, xiii, 64, 111
Freedom
  academic, 11
  autonomous, 2–7, 12
  of conscience, 18, 22
  deliberative, 2–12
  dimensions of, 9
  exercise of, 2–9, 11, 12
  human, xv, 2, 6, 8, 12
  individual, 2–8, 11, 12, 18, 22
  of movement, 105
  negative, 3, 6
  of others, 3, 6, 8
  positive, 3
  rational, 6
  religion, of, 18, 22
  religious, 5
  university, xv, 11
Freedoms, xv, 2–12, 18, 20, 22, 36, 40, 103, 105
Friendship
  act of, 33–35
  ethical, 35
  genuine, 34
  idea of, 33
  notion of (*see* Notion, of friendship)

G
God
  pleasure of, 101
  in service of, x, 109–111
  words of, 92
Gratitude
  account of, 29, 36
  based on virtue, 35
  circle of, 29
  conceptions of, 27
  concept of, 29, 36
  debt of, 28
  democratic form of, x
  express, 27, 29–31, 36
  extensions of, 112
  genuine, 34, 35
  giver of, 35
  humane, x
  practice of, 27, 33, 36
  receiver of, 35
  reciprocate, 35
  reciprocated, 34
  returned, 34–36
  returning, 34
  show, x, 29, 31, 34, 35, 112
  showing, 28–31, 33–35
  shown, 32–34, 36
  surge of, 36
  understanding of, 34

H
Hads, 84–86, 88
Higher education, x, 30, 52
  engagement in, x
Human
  action, 3, 40, 69, 86, 106
  actions, 2, 67, 73, 106, 110, 111
  activity, 11, 68
  acts, 16, 20–25, 73
  agency, 2, 12, 72

INDEX

beings, 54–57, 66, 68, 72, 73, 75–78, 84, 86–88, 93, 96, 102, 105, 110, 112
capacity, 66–69
co-dependence, 11
cognition, 83
confrontation, 41
contestation, 41
cooperation, 95, 105
discernment, 95
emotions, 40, 110
encounter (*see* Encounter, human)
encounters (*see* Encounter, human)
engagement, 2, 16, 92, 97, 109, 110
events, 67
flourishing, 55, 58
freedom, xv, 2, 6, 12
intellect, 82, 83, 85
interpretation, 102
intuitive intelligence, 86, 88
judgements, 63
knowledge, 67, 83, 84
perfect, 71–78
practices, xiii, 20, 28
relations, xiii, xv, 11, 55, 69, 106
relationships, 111
rights, 18–20, 57
self, 81
spirit, 106
Humanity
common, 110
cultivate, x, 29, 57
Humans, x, xvi, 2, 6, 8, 11, 19, 20, 25, 28, 33, 41, 47, 54–58, 65–67, 69, 72–74, 76, 77, 83, 87, 88, 92, 95, 103–106, 110–113
autonomous, 2

I
Ibadah, x, 109–114
Identity
professional, 4
religious, 4, 5, 24
Ijma, 100, 104, 105
Ijtihad, xv, 100–107
Imagination
eye of, 76
narrative, 57
Imagine, 9, 53, 54, 56, 57, 85–87
Inclusiveness, 17, 18
Indebtedness, x, 31, 66
Ingratitude
act of, 28
of students, 32, 33
Injustice, 6, 7, 25, 41, 45, 67, 68, 111, 113
systemic, 45
Innatism
theory of, 82
Intellect
active, 83
human (*see* Human, intellect)
material, 83
potential, 83
Intellectual
exertion, 100, 101, 103, 105
insight, 45
Intelligence, 20, 25, 86, 88
active, 84
Interpretation
fresh, 101, 103
rigid, 104
spiritual, 103
Intimidation
intellectual, 43
Intolerance, 106, 113
Intuition
of being, 83–86
conception of, 82
mystical, 76
of the self, 87
Islam
pillar of, 111
politics in, 100
sources of, 106
traditional, 82

Islamic
  discourse, 100
  epistemology, 62–66
  faith, ix
  law, 101–103
  philosophy, 65, 78
  religious content, 64
  sciences, 72
  tradition, 72
Iteration
  deliberative, xiv, 12
  democratic, 17–25
  practice of, 16

J
Judgement
  compassionate, 55
  deliberative, 9, 11
  emotive (*see* Emotive, judgements)
  errors in, 77
  ethical, 11, 12
  eudaimonistic, 51
  ill-conceived, 74
  independent, 3, 92
  independent human, 103
  plausible, 67
  prudent, 77
  rational, xvi, 12
  repetitive, 20
Justice
  acting with, xi, 109
  act of, 110–114
  democratic, 6, 18, 19, 50, 56–58
  quest for, 102
Justification
  mutual, 9, 10
  of reasons, xvi

K
Knowledge
  basis for, 83
  beneficial, 75
  construction, 95–97
  direct, 76
  intuitive, 85
  of myself, 86
  self-, 75
  source of, 83, 96
  theory of, 82–83
  of the self, 75, 86
  unmediated, 76

L
Learning
  co- (*see* Co-learning)
  form of, 77
Liberty
  cultural, 41
  individual, 3, 6
  negative, 12
  positive, 12
Love, xiii, 28, 29, 33–35, 55, 106
  practices of, 64

M
Madrassa
  curricula, 63
  education, 62, 63
  system, 62
Meaning
  elaboration of, 95
  origin of, 17
  original, 16, 18, 20
  transformed, 16, 19
Moral
  authority, 45
  autonomy, 65
  behaviour, 65
  beliefs, 42, 45
  conflict, 43
  deliberation (*see* Deliberation, moral)
  dialogue, 41
  distress, 40–43

engagement, 45
friction, 42
injury, 44, 45
personality, 65
responsibility, 45
teachings, 65
truth, 41, 43, 46
uncertainty, 42
wrong, 45
Morality, 63–65
  behavioral, 63
Muslim
  community, 64, 101, 102, 104, 105
  education, 62–64, 106
  philosophy, 113, 114
  scholar, 92
  scholars, xv, xvi
  scholarship, xv
  society, 101
  students, 65

N
National
  drama, 22
  trauma, 22
Norms
  Anglo-Saxon, 22, 24
  colonialist, 16
  human rights, 19, 25
  white, 16
Notion
  of being, 112
  of being and thinking, 96
  of belligerence, xiv
  of compassion, 50
  of deliberative freedom, 12
  of democratic education, xiv, xv, 87
  of democratic engagement, 11
  of democratic iterations, 19, 21
  of education, 82
  of friendship, 33, 34

of 'general education,' 66
of gratitude, 36
of *hads*, 85
of *ibadah*, 111, 114
of *ijma*, 105
of *ijtihad*, 102
of intuition, 81–88
of *ma'rifah*, 87
of *paideia*, 66
of paradise, 74
of rationality, 52
of reason, 100
of religion, 100
of sameness and agreement, 93
of *shura*, 91–98
of *ta'dib*, 66, 68
of *tahkayyal*, 85
of 'the perfect human,' 74, 78
of the *tabula rasa*, 83

O
Origin, 6, 8, 17, 24, 56, 73, 83, 102
  countries of, 3, 112

P
Pedagogic
  pilgrimage, xv
  practices, xv
Pedagogical
  encounters, 40, 97
  practices, xiv
Pedagogy, xiii, xiv, 39, 52, 96
  classroom, 52
  critical, 39
  doctoral, 52
Philosophy
  analytic, 54, 114
  of education, xi, xv, 3, 40, 53, 54, 114
  Muslim, 65, 113, 114
  Western, 113

Political
  obligation, 29, 30, 36
  symbol, 24
Practice
  of acting justly, 111
  deliberative, 97
  of democratic education, 36, 50, 74
  dialectical, 5
  emotive, 28–30
  of gratitude, 27, 33
  of *ibadah*, 110
  of *ijtihad*, 102, 106
  of iteration, 16
  narcissistic, 111
  of *shura*, 94, 96
  of worship, 112
Practices
  of *adab*, 63
  of assent, 96
  dehumanising, 16
  demeaning, 24
  democratic, 9, 56, 77
  democratic educational, 40, 77, 87, 88
  of democratic engagement, 96
  education, 53–56
  educational, 67
  enabling, 106
  ethical, 64
  of examination, 18
  of exclusion, 22
  human, 20, 28
  human (*see* Human, practices)
  institutional, 24
  of love, 64
  normative, 96
  pedagogic (*see* Pedagogic, practices)
  pedagogical (*see* Pedagogical, practices)
  regulatory, 24
  supervision, 52
  of worship, 111
Prejudice, 55, 106
Prophet Muhammad, 62, 63, 66, 72

Public
  argument, 17, 19, 24
  defensiveness, 18–20
  deliberation, 17, 55, 104, 110
  discourse, 23
  exchange, 17, 19
  expression of action, 20
  expression of opinion, 20
  self-reflection, 18, 20
  sphere, 17, 18, 18n1, 21–23, 25, 29

R
Racism, 16, 41
Rational, xv, xvi, 6, 11, 12, 19, 25, 40, 52, 58, 72, 76, 84–86, 88, 92, 110
  argumentation, 19, 58
  dimension, 69, 85
  engagement, 88
  reasoning, 76
Rationality
  deliberative, 12, 18
  principles of, 19
Reason
  eye of, 76
  notion of, 100
  practical, 56
  sense of, 17
Reasonableness, ix, xiii, xiv
Reasoning, 47, 57, 76, 83, 85, 105
  power, 84
Reciprocity, 36, 37
  egalitarian, 18, 19
Recognition, xiv, 8, 11, 22, 28, 29, 47, 55, 57, 58, 63, 75, 86, 94, 96, 105, 106
  mutual, 29, 56
Reinterpretation, 95, 103, 106
Relations, xiii–xv, 2, 4, 8, 11, 12, 16, 21, 23, 28–30, 34–37, 41, 50–53, 55, 58, 63–66, 71, 75–78, 82, 84, 85, 87, 88, 96, 97, 100, 104–106, 111, 112

human (*see* Human, relations)
Relationship, x, 9, 31, 35–37, 41, 46, 52, 55, 56, 58, 65, 72, 110, 111
  with God, 73, 112
Relationships
  caring, 52
  enjoyable, 31
  inequitable, x
  productive, 31
  respectful, 31, 56
Religion, 4, 6, 12, 15, 18, 21, 22, 56, 66, 82, 100
Religious
  symbolisms, 22
  views, 5
Respect
  moral, 18
  mutual, 10, 19, 20, 46, 47
Rights, 5–7, 17–21, 23, 24, 29, 41, 46, 47, 57, 58, 64, 67, 76–78, 93, 94, 96, 102
  individual, 4, 18, 22

S
Self-constitution, 23
Shura, xv, 91–98, 100, 105
Social
  activism, 64
  interaction, 56, 63
Socialisation, 7, 27, 61, 62, 64
Sphere
  political, 29, 97
  private, 29, 97
  public, 17, 18, 18n1, 21–23, 25, 29
Spiritual
  emancipation, 103
  ethos, 105
  insight, 72
  interpretation, 103
Spirituality
  act of, 110
  acts of, 103
Students
  doctoral, 51, 58

success, 52
vulnerable (*see* Vulnerable, students)
Supervision
  doctoral, 30, 52, 58
  modes of, 52
  postgraduate, 52
  practices, 52
  student, 31, 32, 50–53
Supervisor, 32, 34, 35, 44, 45, 50–52, 54, 55, 57, 58

T
Tabula rasa, 82, 83
  theory, 83
Tarbiyyah, 64
Teaching
  bad, xiv
  good, xiv
  and learning, x, xiv, 9, 31, 39, 96
Thankful, 34, 35
Thankfulness, 28, 33–35
Think, ix, 2, 9, 36, 45, 56, 63, 68, 83, 86, 87, 94, 97, 112, 113
Thought
  independent, 92
  Muslim, 100, 114
  political, 100–104
  traditions of, xi, 114
Tolerance, xiv, 46

V
Values, 11, 17, 21, 29, 42, 47, 53, 62, 63, 65, 97, 101
  moral, 28, 62, 63
Virtue, ix, 9, 11, 35, 41, 62, 88
Vulnerability, 50, 52, 54, 55, 57, 58, 113
Vulnerable, 50, 56
  students, 53

W
Western tradition, ix

Printed in the United States
By Bookmasters